M000267729

CROSSING PUGET SOUND

FROM BLACK BALL STEAMER TO WASHINGTON STATE FERRIES

STEVEN J. PICKENS

AMERICA
THROUGH TIME®
ADDING COLOR TO AMERICAN HISTORY

America Through Time is an imprint of Fonthill Media LLC
www.through-time.com
office@through-time.com

Published by Arcadia Publishing by arrangement with Fonthill Media LLC
For all general information, please contact Arcadia Publishing:
Telephone: 843-853-2070
Fax: 843-853-0044
E-mail: sales@arcadiapublishing.com
For customer service and orders:
Toll-Free 1-888-313-2665

www.arcadiapublishing.com

First published 2019

ISBN 978-1-63499-153-7

Typeset in 10pt on 13pt Sabon
Printed and bound in England

CONTENTS

ACKNOWLEDGMENTS

No one writes a book alone, and I'd like to thank the following people for their help in putting this book together: Brandon Moser, Matt Masuoka, Zack Heistand, Shawn J. Dake, Randy Flodquist, Jason Leander, Jason Slotemaker, Mike Byrne, Mike Bonkowski, Brandon Swan, and Gloria Mairs for the use of their photos and research; the Belvedere-Tiburon Landmarks Society for their donation of several key photos to my collection; the collection of Captains Raymond W. and Bill Hughes, whose clippings tied up many missing links.

Special thanks to the researchers who came before me—Harre Demoro, Gordon Newell, Joe Williamson, M. S. Kline, George Bayless, Michael Skalley, and Jim Faber.

NOTES

All photos are in the author's collection unless otherwise noted. All colorization has been done by the author. Colorized photos are specifically noted; all other photos are original color.

The Puget Sound Navigation Company will be referred to either as PSN or by its more informal name, the Black Ball Line or simply Black Ball. Washington State Ferries will be abbreviated to WSF.

For the sake of brevity, the photos donated by the Belvedere-Tiburon Landmarks Society will appear abbreviated as BTLS.

This is by no means intended to be a fully comprehensive catalog of every single vessel to ply Puget Sound and the Salish Sea; such an endeavor would comprise several lengthy volumes. Much of the material either was unavailable for use or simply didn't exist. Therefore, the focus is on some of the more well-known vessels and those steamers which were instrumental in the development of auto ferry service on Puget Sound. The author offers his heart-felt apologies if your favorite vessel was omitted.

INTRODUCTION

Crossing Puget Sound today on one of the behemoths of the Washington State Ferries fleet, say the *Tacoma*, it is hard to believe that such a large vessel could trace its lineage back to humble beginnings. Indeed, the *Tacoma*'s namesake, a crack Puget Sound Navigation steamer, would have been dwarfed by the modern ferry.

For more than two decades, Puget Sound was crisscrossed by a fleet of tidy, fast passenger steamers, so numerous that they became known as the "Mosquito Fleet." They carried names such as *Dix, Arcadia, Kitsap, Nisqually,* and *Utopia,* and numbered into the hundreds. These steamers transported people and goods from small hamlets and towns up and down the Sound to major population centers like Seattle, Olympia, Tacoma, and Bellingham. The waters of Western Washington were the easiest way to get from place to place, a natural made super highway, and soon there was no shortage of vessels to transport both people and goods from one port to another. Most of the steamers were small, quite unassuming little vessels compared to the "pocket liners" of the Canadian Pacific Line steaming down from Canada; all of them were made of wood, which was in ready supply. As the years progressed and shipbuilding facilities improved, the Mosquito Fleet ranged from utilitarian in both design and fittings to downright posh.

The Puget Sound Navigation Company, founded in 1898 by Charles Peabody, was a subsidiary of the Alaska Steamship Company. By 1903, the company would emerge as the dominant transportation company on Puget Sound when it merged with the LaConner Trading and Transport Company, which immediately increased the fleet by twenty ships. That same year, the company built the *Clallam*, a luxurious, forty-four-stateroom passenger steamer for the Seattle-Victoria run.

Unfortunately, during a violent storm, the *Clallam* sank with a loss of fifty-six lives. As a direct result of this, PSN decided against building any more wooden-hulled steamers. The steel-hulled steamers *Iroquois, Chippewa* and *Indianapolis* were purchased from the Great Lakes and brought around South America for use on Puget Sound immediately, while the company built a quintet of iron-hulled steamers which would culminate in the *Tacoma* of 1913. The *Tacoma* would not only become the fastest steamer on Puget Sound, but was allegedly the fastest steamer of her type propelled by a single screw (propeller) in the world.

In the years leading up to the First World War, these steamers with their bright red smokestacks would traverse Puget Sound: *Kulshan* cruising between Bellingham and Seattle, *Potlatch* steaming up and down Hood Canal, *Sol Duc* sailing from Seattle to Victoria via Port Townsend and Port Angeles, *Sioux* sailing between Seattle, Irondale, Port Townsend, and Everett, and the two-stacked express steamer *Tacoma*, which sailed between Tacoma and Seattle at a pace faster than traffic on Interstate 5 can now make on most days.

And then, abruptly, after World War I, the Mosquito Fleet began to go extinct. Steamer after steamer vanished, for the automobile was now taking over as the prominent mode of transportation, and federal funds were building and improving roads throughout the entire region.

Puget Sound Navigation, which had already started scooping up smaller companies and would become a virtual monopoly by the 1930s, found itself with a fleet of vessels that were rapidly becoming obsolete.

At first, cars were hauled in some of the steamers which had portions of their cargo areas and passenger cabins hastily emptied out to carry a few autos between ports. This was accomplished on the *Sol Duc,* for example, but not effectively. The cumbersome process to load autos on and off the steamer often included deflating the tires in order for the car to clear the overhead deck, then manually pushing the vehicle on board. The process was repeated in reverse upon landing, taking a great deal of time.

It was clear something had to be done, and PSN started an ambitious program to adapt their current fleet to meet the demands of the post-war traveling public. They started with their wooden steamers, which were more quickly adaptable than their iron counterparts. Beginning in 1918, with the purchase of the old stern-wheeler *Bailey Gatzert*, steamers such as the *Kitsap II*, *City of Angeles,* and the *Whatcom* would be rebuilt, retaining their steam plants but having their hulls widened and their cabins lifted to accommodate cars.

The results were somewhat mixed, because while the vessels were now adapted to vehicle traffic, many of the docks were not. The solution for vessels like the *City of Angeles* and *Whatcom,* now the *City of Bremerton* after her conversion in 1921, was to be fitted with the ungainly Barlow steam elevators to lift the cars off the ferry to the height of the docks which had been at the passenger cabin level of the steamers. Transporting vehicles itself had improved, but the time offloading hadn't, and in very rapid order docks were modified. The elevators vanished and cleaner, more modern looking vessels, something that could be easily more defined as a "ferry," emerged.

The wooden steamer conversions having proved successful, PSN now tackled some of the iron-hulled vessels. *Sioux* retained most of her classic steamship lines and looks and emerged in 1924 as *Olympic* for the route across the Strait of Juan de Fuca to Victoria; she would later be joined by a completely rebuilt *Iroquois*, which handled the "night route" from Seattle to Port Townsend and Port Angeles and Victoria for overnight travelers in 1928. 1924 also saw the conversion of the former *H. B. Kennedy*, already having been renamed *Seattle*, converted into a luxurious car ferry for the Bremerton route.

The most ambitious conversion was that of the *Chippewa* in 1926. Pulled from mothballs where she had been since the end of the war, the steamer was rebuilt as the company flagship to accommodate ninety cars and 2000 passengers, becoming the largest car ferry on the west coast.

By 1928, Captain Alexander Peabody had taken over the running of the company after his father Charles had passed away. He reinstated the iconic company flag from the days when the Peabody family ran packet ships from the east coast to Liverpool—a crimson field with a black ball. The Puget Sound Navigation Company retained the more formal sounding name, but the company became known as the Black Ball Line forever after.

And still the traffic continued to grow. The company grew with it and continued to build, expand, and rebuild its existing fleet. *Kitsap II*, already rebuilt as the *City of Bellingham*, would be rebuilt a second time, given a plush passenger cabin with a full-service dining room, and become the steam ferry *Quilcene*, sailing through the picturesque San Juan Islands and to Sidney, British Columbia. *Chippewa* would be rebuilt again in 1932 with even more luxurious accommodations, but most importantly repowered with a direct-drive Busch-Sulzer diesel engine.

It wasn't long before Captain Peabody realized that diesel was far cheaper to run and maintain than steam. At the start of the Depression, his eclectic fleet contained many steamer conversions, small and increasingly uneconomical vessels that were costing exponentially more each year to maintain.

Black Ball, which hadn't been in the habit of building its own vessels since before the war, would soon be given a huge opportunity. But before that happened, a 1928-built turbine-electric vessel would suffer a catastrophic fire and would rise phoenix-like from the ashes to become perhaps one of the most well-known ferries in the world.

Captain Peabody snapped up the burnt-out wreck of San Francisco Bay's Key System ferry *Peralta* with an idea of building his new flagship. Originally conceived to be a larger version of the *Chippewa*, sometime in 1934, plans changed. The new ferry would emerge as the aluminum-painted, streamlined ferry *Kalakala* in July of 1935, and would dazzle passengers and tourists alike for nearly thirty years.

The *Kalakala* would end up being the last, almost-new-built ferry for the company for over a decade. San Francisco began retiring nearly its entire fleet starting in 1937, put out of work by the new cross-Bay bridges, and Black Ball began snapping up the idled ferries. One by one, the converted steamers would disappear. By 1939, nearly all the steel-hulled steamers were gone.

Labor strife and strikes hit the company after World War II. State ownership seemed all but inevitable, and while Captain Peabody celebrated the construction of his William F. Gibbs-designed "night boat" *Chinook* in 1947, continued disputes with state government resulted in all Black Ball vessels being tied up, shutting traffic down on Puget Sound for nearly three weeks. Negotiations would continue for several years, but the state won out and Captain Peabody's company would cease operations on June 1, 1951. Not one to be thwarted, Captain Peabody would take a handful of vessels and start over in Canada, essentially starting modern ferry operations in British Columbia.

Red and black stacks were replaced with green, white and black, and Washington State Ferries was born. They continued to operate Captain Peabody's eclectic mix of steam and diesel, wood and steel-hulled ferries purchased from San Francisco for several decades to come. The last of steam vessels would retire in 1969; the last of the wooden fleet would be retired in 1980; the last of the San Francisco ferries, the 1927-built Steel Electrics, would finally be retired in 2007.

Over the years, the state added new boats, purchased some used from other places, and started and ultimately abandoned a passenger-only fleet. The skyline of Seattle has changed, but the scenery from Mount Baker in the north to Mount Rainer in the south has not, and with few exceptions, the routes haven't changed much either.

Puget Sound today is every bit the essential highway it was long before steamers ever arrived on its waters, when tribes would move from location to location in canoes. If anything, its importance has grown over the decades, not only as vital link for trade, commerce, and transportation, but also recreation as each summer brings a fleet of mammoth cruise ships.

Crossing Puget Sound today, it is impossible not to sense the great history of its most iconic form of transportation, the fleet of ferryboats that once started from a mismatched collection of converted steamships.

Travel by water has never been more prominent or necessary than it is today. In 2018, nearly *25 million* commuters, tourists, and travelers traversed Puget Sound by ferry. The ferries remain the number one tourist draw in the State of Washington.

The green and white fleet of Washington State Ferries, picturesque yet practical, are still every bit as crucial to transportation needs in Washington State as those red-stacked, clunky conversions which first appeared over 100 years ago. The size and livery may have changed, but the goals remain the same: safe, reliable passage on the Puget Sound Highway.

1

SOUTH PUGET SOUND

The south end of Puget Sound is characterized by its many passages and inlets, and everywhere on the horizon, the towering, glacier-clad presence of Mount Rainier.

For decades the southern Puget Sound ferry routes were synonymous with Pierce County, the governing body that controlled all but the direct route from Tacoma to Seattle. Today, the county still maintains one run, while Washington State Ferries has the only other remaining south Sound route: the 1.7-mile crossing between Tahlequah on Vashon Island and Point Defiance in Tacoma. And how it got it is a bit of a circuitous path.

PIERCE COUNTY AND THE WASHINGTON NAVIGATION COMPANY–ALL POINTS SOUTH

These two routes are what remains of the dozen or so different ferry stops, all of them run by the Skansie Brothers' Washington Navigation Company. Under Washington Navigation, which operated under charter for Pierce County, the *Skansonia* served Tahlequah on Vashon Island and the *Defiance* sailed to Gig Harbor, both from Tacoma's Point Defiance. From 6th Avenue at Titlow Beach (west of downtown Tacoma), the *Fox Island* (ex-*Wollochet*) served Fox Island and East Cromwell on the Kitsap Peninsula while the *City of Tacoma* and *Gig Harbor* carried cars to Point Fosdick, just south of where the Tacoma Narrows Bridges stand today. Furthest south, the *City of Steilacoom* provided crossings from Steilacoom to Anderson Island, McNeil Island, and Longbranch.

Nearly all the vessels on south Puget Sound had been built by the Skansie Shipbuilding Company. Known for their speed and efficiency (the *Skansonia*, from keel laying to first day in service, was accomplished in just twelve weeks), the company would produce such long-lived vessels as the *Defiance, Skansonia, Wollochet, Vashonia*, and many others. They picked up the *City of Tacoma* and *Gig Harbor* secondhand.

THE DEPRESSION AND THE TACOMA NARROWS BRIDGE

Pierce County managed all the ferry traffic in the south Puget Sound, but didn't actually own or operate the vessels, contracting with the Washington Navigation Company to provide the ferries and the crews. From the company's founding in 1922 until the start of the Depression, the operation worked very successfully. As the Depression deepened, the company began losing money, even with the county subsidy. In 1935, they petitioned to restructure under federal bankruptcy laws. The company had been dealt a huge financial blow when they'd been ordered to pay back $126,000 (equivalent to over two million dollars in 2019) in subsidies that the county council hadn't had the legal authority to pay. The company won the right to reorganize, but the damage had been done. Pierce County purchased their own ferry for operating to Anderson and McNeil Islands and contracted the Olson family to operate it. In 1939, the *Tahoma,* built for the Olson family, joined the county's *Pioneer*, cutting the Washington Navigation Company out of the route entirely. The county would purchase the *City of Steilacoom* at the same time, running it to Fox Island, and reducing the Washington Navigation Company's operation to the runs departing Point Defiance to Tahlequah and Gig Harbor. Bigger trouble for the company was on the horizon with the completion of the first Tacoma Narrows Bridge.

The notorious "Galloping Gertie" opened in July of 1940. At once, the ferry route from Gig Harbor became obsolete, and put the Washington Navigation Company out of business. However, no one realized on that sunny July day that four months later the span would be at the bottom of the Narrows. A fatal design flaw caused the collapse during a storm on November 7, 1940. Due to the intervention of the Second World War, the bridge would not be rebuilt for another decade. Ferry service was needed once again, and in a hurry.

As it had been a state highway that had collapsed, the State of Washington was tasked with restoring ferry service. They purchased the *Defiance, City of Tacoma,* and *Skansonia* from the Washington Navigation Company. The ferries were operated for the state first by the Washington Navigation Company in a similar agreement as had been done with Pierce County; the Point Defiance-Tahlequah route was purchased by Black Ball in 1941. Less than two years later, the Washington Navigation Company was gone, and the Puget Sound Navigation Company took over the state's charter for the Gig Harbor route, cementing its presence on south Puget Sound. Black Ball would continue to run the ferries for the state between Gig Harbor and Point Defiance until the new Narrows Bridge opened in 1950, although the *City of Tacoma* would be pulled out of service by the United States Coast Guard in 1949 because of its low freeboard.

The Skansie family sold off its remaining vessels. The *Fox Island* was purchased by Horluck Transportation Company, running the route between Port Orchard and the Puget Sound Naval Shipyard. After World War II ended, the traffic to the shipyard drastically declined and the *Fox Island* was sold in 1947 to the newly formed Olympic Ferries Inc., reestablishing the Port Townsend-Keystone run that Black Ball had abandoned in 1943.

Defiance would be sold by the State of Washington along with the *City of Tacoma* in April of 1951, mere months before Washington State Ferries was established—both at a huge loss. The *Defiance* would replace the *Fox Island* for Olympic Ferries and hold that route until 1971; the *City of Tacoma* would never work as a ferry again, and eventually sink off Yarrow Point on Lake Washington where her remains lie to this day.

The *Skansonia*, however, remained a state asset and in 1951 took on the green and white livery of Washington State Ferries. A small vessel with an appallingly slow speed (about 8 knots), she would stay in south Puget Sound waters on the short crossing for which she was best suited. For the next sixteen years, the *Skansonia* called the Point Defiance-Tahlequah route home.

The *Hiyu*, a steel vessel built specifically for the route by Washington State Ferries, would retire the venerable *Skansonia* in 1967. The *Hiyu*'s size would eventually put it off the run as well, first to be replaced by the *Olympic* and then for a twenty-year stretch by the former Baltimore ferry *Rhododendron*. The *Rhody*, as she was affectionately known, sailed the route for nearly twenty years when, at age sixty-five, she was retired in 2012.

The *Chetzemoka*, built in 2010 and the second vessel of that name for Washington State Ferries, holds down the Point Defiance-Tahlequah route today.

Further south, Pierce County still owns the ferries that cross from Steilacoom to Anderson and Ketron Islands. *Pioneer*, built in 1916, lasted until 1966, and was replaced by the former Astoria-Megler ferry *Tourist No. 2* which was renamed *Islander*. The little *Tahoma* carried on as backup boat until 1976 when the first *Steilacoom*, a former Navy vessel originally named *Aquidneck*, replaced her. *Islander* was retired with the addition of the all-steel ferry *Christine Anderson* in 1994. *Steilacoom II* replaced the *Steilacoom* in 2006 for a short time. Washington State Ferries ended up chartering the *Steilacoom II* on the Port Townsend-Keystone run when the Steel Electric class vessels were pulled out of service in 2007. The boat sailed for several years until the *Chetzemoka* was ready in 2010.

DEFUNCT ROUTE: SEATTLE-TACOMA

Once the most popular route on the South Sound was the run between Tacoma and Seattle. For many years, fierce competition and even some races between steamers happened on the route, until like all the other routes, Black Ball bought out the competition.

After WWI, with better roads between the port cities, the route, while still popular, saw its traffic decline. The *Tacoma* held down the run, paired with the *Indianapolis* or the *Washington*. The *Washington* had been the fast steamer *Flyer* and at one point had been Black Ball's biggest competitor on the route. Both the steamers were proving to be inadequate for the run, mainly in terms of passenger comfort, so the *H. B. Kennedy* was removed from the Bremerton route, remodeled, and renamed *Seattle* to run opposite the *Tacoma*.

The *Seattle* did not stay on the route for long. The *Indianapolis* moved to the Bremerton run and set off a series of complaints and lawsuits about her heavy wake along the shores of Rich Passage. The *Seattle*, which did not have the same wake issues, spent more time on the Bremerton route, leaving the *Tacoma* to carry on with the aging *Indianapolis* on the Tacoma-Seattle route.

Traffic finally dropped so low on the Seattle-Tacoma route that Black Ball shut the run down in December of 1930. The *Indianapolis* would be rebuilt as an auto ferry two years later, while the speedy *Tacoma* would on occasion work the Bremerton run or run excursions to Victoria. Both vessels would be scrapped in 1938-39.

Interestingly, studies are now being conducted on reviving the old run between Tacoma and Seattle with passenger-only fast ferries. The idea is not without merit, as there would likely be a great number of people who would prefer a comfortable trip up the Puget Sound highway rather than being stuck in traffic on Interstate 5.

LONG BRANCH---McNEIL and ANDERSON ISLANDS via STEILACOOM

Ferry from Steilacoom to the islands and Long Branch, and you are in a country of countless trees and uncrowded beaches. Catch some lake trout on Anderson Island and camp in the open. Visit McNeil Island, see the remarkable Federal prison farm that turns out such splendid men. Then through Long Branch strike out on the main roads, first enjoying the waters of Lake Bay, Joe's Bay and Delano Beach.

POINT FOSDICK---SIXTH AVENUE

A short, quick ferry route to Hood Canal and Peninsula highways. Pt. Fosdick always has good fishing. There are boats and cabins to rent, an extensive campground, and an excellent tea room. A pebbly beach appeals to young and old---picnic here some time.

FOX ISLAND---EAST CROMWELL--- SIXTH AVENUE

On Fox Island and around East Cromwell are summer camps that offer all the quiet beauty of outdoors, a short distance from Tacoma. Good roads and trails abound and intrigue you into fascinating woodland that opens out on cool beaches everywhere.

Right: "You are in a country of countless trees and uncrowded beaches," promoted the Washington Navigation Company in this brochure from the 1930s, and their boats would take you there.

Below: The *Steilacoom,* formerly the *YFB-14 Aquidneck*, called the Anderson Island route home for over three decades until retired by the *Steilacoom II.* The retired Navy ferry had sailed between Newport, RI and Goat Island.

Renamed *Point Ruston*, the old *Steilacoom* is now a floating showroom in Tacoma. *[Courtesy of Matt Masuoka]*

The *Steilacoom II* spent its early life sailing "on loan" to Washington State Ferries after the Steel Electrics were abruptly pulled from service in 2007. "Bob," as crews called the keelless ferry, handled poorly even in moderate seas. The ferry was returned to Pierce County in 2010.

Above: The *Islander* was the former Astoria-Megler ferry *Tourist No. 2*. After spending years as the *Kirkland* for Argosy Cruises, she was damaged by fire and sold. After repairs were made, the ferry, under her original name, returned to Astoria in 2016 and is undergoing restoration.

Right: Until the Tacoma Narrows Bridge, south Puget Sound was the domain of the Skansie Brothers' Washington Navigation Company. Their vessels (and brochures) would long outlive the company, which collapsed into bankruptcy in 1940.

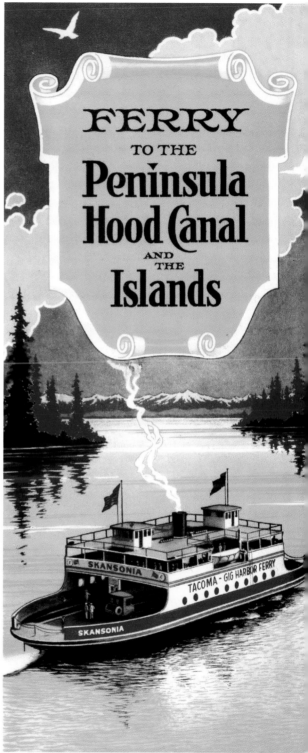

FERRY TO THE Peninsula Hood Canal AND THE Islands

The steamer *Tacoma* sailed for years on the Tacoma-Seattle route. Hailed as the "fastest single-screw [propeller] steamer in the world," the arrow-like vessel regularly sailed faster than her billed 22 knots. Shut down after roads opened between the two cities, there has been recent talk of reactivating the route with passenger ferries.

After the Tacoma-Seattle run ended, the *Tacoma* would fill in as needed on the Bremerton route or turned to excursion trips to Victoria. Seen here cruising through Deception Pass, the crack steamer is en route to Victoria. Once the pride of the Black Ball fleet, the steamer was scrapped in 1938. *(Colorized)*

The *City of Tacoma* ended up as state property in 1940. Slated to continue service under Washington State Ferries, the vessel became a sudden albatross to the State when the Coast Guard deemed to her have "dangerously low freeboard." The ferry was sold in 1951 at a huge loss.

Vessels on the Point Defiance-Tahlequah became known for their longevity on the route. The *Skansonia*, already state property in 1951, stayed there after becoming part of the Washington State Ferries fleet. Too slow to be used elsewhere (a whopping 8 knots, maximum), she remained on the route until replaced by the *Hiyu* in 1967.

Today, the *Skansonia* is moored on Lake Union, a popular venue for weddings. The Skansie Brothers' ferry, which took 12 weeks to build from start to finish, will celebrate her 90th birthday in 2019. *[Courtesy of Matt Masuoka]*

The *Hiyu* arrived in 1967. Originally registered with a capacity of 40 cars, changing regulations and additional safety equipment over the years whittled this down to 34. In the crunch between building cycles, the little ferry would often be called in to routes to fill in during emergencies—34 cars being moved across the water being better than none. She's seen here arriving at Point Defiance in the early 1970s. *[Courtesy of the Captain Raymond W. Hughes Collection]*

Retired in 2016, the *Hiyu* was sold and reborn as a successful floating entertainment venue. She can be found on Lake Union, available for all kinds of events. *[Courtesy of Zack Heistand]*

A rare color photo of the *Rhododendron* in her original livery and name, the *Governor Herbert R. O'Conor* in Baltimore, sailing past the bridge that would soon surplus her. Snapped up by WSF, she joined the fleet in the early 1950s, assigned to the Hood Canal run. Later the ferry would work at Mukilteo-Clinton and the Port Townsend-Keystone run before being assigned to Point Defiance-Tahlequah. Today she's in Fanny Bay, Canada, a processing platform for shellfish.

Last day of service for the *Rhododendron*, 23 January 2012. Named for the state flower, she was also the last ferry in the fleet to have portholes on her car deck. *[Courtesy of Matt Masuoka]*

Olympic, second ferry of that name on Puget Sound, also ended her career on the Point Defiance-Tahlequah run. She was moved to the short (1.7 miles) Point Defiance route after suffering a mechanical failure on the Port Townsend run, which left her adrift, having only one engine. The Coast Guard decided that situation was no longer acceptable for the route. Seen here in September 1990, the ferry was in her last few years of service.

Moored at Ketron Island (though more commonly on beach, depending on the tide), the *Olympic* is now being slowly dismantled by her owner. *[Courtesy of Matt Masuoka]*

Chetzemoka, second ferry of that name on Puget Sound waters, now holds down the Point Defiance-Tahlequah run. Originally intended for the Port Townsend run, she is filled with historic photos of that port city. She was moved due to her propulsion system, which is different from sisters *Kennewick* and *Salish* and is, according WSF, less maneuverable than the newer sisters, hence her reassignment. *[Courtesy of Matt Masuoka]*

2

CENTRAL PUGET SOUND

FAUNTLEROY-VASHON-SOUTHWORTH, SEATTLE-BREMERTON, SEATTLE-BAINBRIDGE ISLAND (WINSLOW), KINGSTON-EDMONDS, MUKILTEO-CLINTON, PORT TOWNSEND-KEYSTONE (COUPEVILLE)

The central Puget Sound routes run roughly from the north end of Vashon Island and stop at the Port Townsend-Keystone (now Coupeville) run. The central Sound encompasses the main population centers of Western Washington, and the largest boats serve these routes.

Today, Washington State Ferries owns and operates all the auto routes. With the start of auto ferry service in the 1920s, the routes were split up among several companies, one by one of which were bought up by Black Ball by the end of the 1930s. Throughout the forties, smaller runs were consolidated or discontinued and, apart from relocating the Harper terminal to Southworth, the state runs the same routes today.

VASHON ISLAND

Service between Vashon Island and Fauntleroy was inaugurated in 1916 by the King County ferry *Robert Bridges*. Originally designed as a passenger-only vessel, it was altered a short time later to carry cars. Officially, auto ferry service to Vashon from Fauntleroy is recorded as beginning in 1919, presumably with the *Robert Bridges*. The ferry was pulled from the run and remodeled and renamed *Mount Vernon* for the Anacortes-Sidney route in 1923.

In 1925, the Kitsap County Transportation Company took over the Fauntleroy end of the route. The company had been operating ferries from Harper on the Kitsap Peninsula near Port Orchard to Vashon Island and downtown Seattle. Fauntleroy had been chosen by residents of Vashon Island over the landing in downtown Seattle for more frequent service—seventeen minutes to Fauntleroy versus an hour to downtown Seattle. The ferry *Washington*, a veteran from Lake Washington service, inaugurated the route. She would soon be displaced by the *Kitsap (I)*, an all-wood diesel ferry completed later that same year.

Black Ball took over the Kitsap County Transportation Company in 1935 and operated the route until the strikes of the late 1940s. Vashon residents, fearing of being beholden to the whims of the Black Ball Line, prevented the *Illahee* from landing at the Vashon Island dock, and thus prevented the company from re-establishing a presence on the island. Legally they were able to establish their own ferry service with a charter to King County, which they soon did. The service began with the decrepit ferry *Lincoln* and then with the newly refurbished *Crosline*.

State ownership established a pattern of longevity on the run for certain vessels. The *Quinault*, for example, was assigned to the Southworth-Vashon-Fauntleroy route not long after the state took ownership in 1951 and stayed there for the next thirty years. In 1958, she was joined by the newly-built *Klahowya*. The Evergreen State Class vessel would establish a record yet to be duplicated in the fleet: continuous service on one route for an astounding fifty-six years. She was moved to the San Juan Islands to work the inter-island route in 2014, retiring in 2017.

Today, the route is serviced by three Issaquah Class vessels—*Issaquah, Cathlamet*, and as of 2019, the *Kitsap*.

SEATTLE-BREMERTON

One of the earliest routes crossing Puget Sound, the Seattle-Bremerton route once comprised a series of smaller routes that were all phased out by the time of State ownership in 1951.

The primary route, however, had always been the direct run from Seattle to Bremerton. The presence of the Puget Sound Naval Shipyard necessitated fast, reliable service.

The old sternwheeler *Bailey Gatzert* is credited as having launched the first auto service on the route in 1918. Only partially converted to carry cars, the arrangement proved cumbersome. In addition, patrons on the route were demanding better vessels more suited to auto service. Black Ball chose the passenger steamer *Whatcom* to be converted into a proper car ferry. The work was finished in 1921, and rechristened *City of Bremerton*, the first real auto ferry went into service on the route. The *Seattle* was added to the route in 1924 after a similar conversion. It was not a new route for the vessel, which had been running to Bremerton since 1909 as the express steamer *H.B. Kennedy*. The ferry was noted for its luxurious passenger accommodations and speed, which had not diminished with her conversion. The *Seattle* could make the crossing in roughly forty-five minutes. The two converted steamers held down the route until the *Chippewa* arrived in 1926. Another former passenger steamer, the *Chippewa* had been idled since before the end of the war. Completely rebuilt, she retained her steam plant and most of her passenger cabin. Licensed for 2,000 passengers and ninety 1926-sized cars, she replaced the smaller *City of Bremerton*.

Traffic on the run continued to build, and *Chippewa* and *Seattle* dominated the run throughout the twenties and into the 1930s. The *Chippewa* was rebuilt again in 1932, her steam plant having proved too slow and costly to run. This time around, her entire passenger cabin was rebuilt, complete with a men's smoking room and ladies' lounge. The cabin was lined with mahogany paneling throughout. Now capable of a fifty-five-minute crossing, the *Chippewa* became the flagship of the fleet—only to be displaced three years later by a shiny upstart.

KALAKALA–SYNONYMOUS WITH THE BREMERTON ROUTE

It is impossible to talk about the Seattle-Bremerton route without mentioning the most famous vessel ever assigned to the route: the streamlined, Art Deco *Kalakala*.

Built on the fire-ravaged hull of the former Key System passenger-only ferry *Peralta*, the "Buck Rogers design" seems to have been nearly an afterthought. Early drawings of the vessel, and indeed the plans that reside at the Library of Congress, show a ferry that looks nearly identical to the *Chippewa*. All the public rooms that would appear on the *Kalakala* are in these 1934 blueprints; the only thing that isn't is the curvaceous appearance of the ferry, which has a tall funnel like the *Chippewa*, no round windows, and no "flying bridge." Perhaps a coincidence or perhaps not, if you take a pencil and round over the profile of the 1934 drawing, the ferry bears a startling resemblance to the finished product.

The designer of the ferry has been lost to time, attributed to many architects over the years, with Boeing's Louis Proctor, who built the model, generally credited for the streamlined design. No one really knows. It's entirely possible Captain Alexander Peabody or his wife, who has also been noted as potentially designing the ferry, looked at the proposed profile drawing, took a pencil and rounded it off.

In any case, the silver-painted streamliner debuted in July 1935 and was an immediate sensation. Newsreels appeared all over the world of the ferry, some praising, others deriding the futuristic look. Everywhere, people were talking about the *Kalakala*—which was exactly what Captain Peabody had hoped for.

Not all the comments were good, however. The streamliner vibrated excessively—so badly that in the galley waitresses only poured coffee cups half-full. Despite the much advertised "eighteen-knot cruising speed," it was closer to sixteen. Commuters complained, wanting to know why they had to be subjected to the vibrating, slower ferry when the *Seattle* not only ran smoothly but was decidedly faster.

In reality, the *Kalakala*'s use as a ferry was very much secondary. She could carry up to 2,000 passengers, true, but her narrow beam at 55 feet would soon cut her carrying capacity down drastically. Her rudder had been shaved down to compensate for her overpowered engine; as a result, steering the vessel was a challenge. The bridge was a navigator's nightmare, as it was impossible to see the front of the vessel from the wheelhouse, and the inch-thick portholes were tilted at an angle that distorted the view. In addition, it seems no one had thought to stiffen the lower deck, which had only been designed for human feet and not heavy automobiles. The support beams were too far apart, and at once the car deck would ripple from the weight of cars driving across it, a trait that stayed with the ferry her entire career.

The *Kalakala* had been very lightly constructed, either as an economy measure or because Captain Peabody didn't have expectations that the ferry would last as long as it did. In any case, leaks were a problem throughout her years, and she became an expensive vessel to maintain. Possibly most telling, when Black Ball was forced out of business in 1951, Captain Peabody made no attempt to hold onto the ferry which, with its enclosed bow, would have made it a seemingly obvious choice for the crossing from the new terminal at Horseshoe Bay to Nanaimo.

Still, the *Kalakala* became a beloved vessel. Patrons loved her "Moonlight Cruises" with live music broadcast from the ship—a venue she'd taken over from the *Chippewa*. Passengers enjoyed the excursions to Victoria in the summer months in the late 1940s. And, when freshly painted, there was nothing on Puget Sound that could match her stunning looks. So unique was that streamlined profile that at the time of the Century 21 World's Fair, some twenty-seven years after her debut, the *Kalakala* was rated as the second most popular tourist draw, falling behind only the brand-new Space Needle.

ALL-TIME HIGH—THE WAR YEARS

As America moved toward WWII, the importance of the Bremerton run became more and more evident as work ramped up at the Puget Sound Naval Shipyard. As early as 1940, it was clear that even with the passenger capacity of the two ferries, they weren't going to be adequate. Having purchased much of the idled San Francisco ferry fleet, the new vessels were placed on the Bremerton run as soon as they were ready for service, starting with the Wood Electrics and then moving on to the faster Steel Electrics. None proved fast enough to maintain the schedule needed, or large enough to handle the passengers. Black Ball rebuilt two of the Steel Electrics as direct-drive, single-ended vessels which, despite having to back into the slip at Bremerton, allowed the vessels to maintain the tight schedules faster than any other ferry at that time and doubled their passenger capacity. The ferries *Santa Rosa* and *Fresno* were the Steel Electric ferries chosen for conversion. Renamed *Enetai* and *Willapa* respectively, they would hold down the run from 1941 until they were retired nearly thirty years later.

Four ferries on the run soon proved not to be up to the task. *Malahat*, the former steam ferry *Napa Valley,* arrived in 1942. It sailed until an errant cigarette caused the passenger cabin to be gutted by fire in March 1943. Rebuilt, she went back on the run, joined later by the *City of Sacramento* for a total of *six* vessels on the route, a record number of vessels never to be duplicated.

After the war, traffic on the Bremerton run began to decline. The route dropped down to three vessels, with two handling traffic in the off season. The main reason for this was the end of the war and the opening of the Agate Pass Bridge between Bainbridge Island and the mainland. This created a more direct route to the northern part of the Kitsap Peninsula and the vacation playground of the Olympic National Forest just beyond.

By 1967, with the state now in the ferry business for over a decade, the single-ended ferries were expensive to maintain and obsolete. With the arrival of the Super Class ferries *Hyak* and *Yakima*, the *Kalakala, Enetai*, and *Willapa* were sold, the latter two returning to San Francisco.

The 1970s brought another economic downturn to the route, and the Super Class Ferries, fuel-thirsty boats in an era of oil embargoes, were replaced by the far more economical Issaquah Class boats. Varying pairings of those vessels would last from the 1980s well into the 1990s, augmented by the passenger-only vessels *Skagit, Kalama, Tyee*, and the high-speed catamarans *Chinook* and *Snohomish*. The passenger-only program, while well intended, never penciled out. The passenger-only boats were also fuel-thirsty and expensive to run. When the major source of Washington State Ferries' funding was cut off in 1999, the passenger only program was phased out, and the vessels sold off a few years later.

The Issaquah Class may have been adequate for car capacity throughout the 1990s but by the end of the decade that was no longer holding true. Whenever WSF placed a larger vessel on the route, traffic increased, drawing commuters from the middle part of Kitsap County. Seattle becoming increasingly expensive to live in, commuting from the other side of the Sound has become even more appealing in the last decade. The smaller Issaquahs on the route were replaced in favor of the Super or Jumbo Class vessels, with the brand-new Olympic Class ferry *Chimacum* arriving on the Bremerton run in 2017.

DEFUNCT ROUTES: ALKI-MANCHESTER, FLETCHER BAY-BROWNSVILLE, POINT WHITE-BREMERTON

Ferries once sailed between Alki Point and Manchester on the Kitsap Peninsula, Seattle and Port Orchard, Seattle and Manchester, and on the Bremerton side, Fletcher Bay and Brownsville and Point White and Bremerton. As connections via roads were made better, most of the smaller runs became redundant, unprofitable, or, in the case of the Alki Point run, the dock was washed out in a storm and never rebuilt. The last car ferry route to be dropped was the Point White-Bremerton run, which happened as soon as Washington State Ferries took over in 1951.

SEATTLE TO BAINBRIDGE ISLAND (WINSLOW)

Far from the bedroom community to Seattle that it is now, Bainbridge Island was once known for its large strawberry farms and rural setting. Few back then would likely have guessed that the route would one day grow to the most-traveled in the fleet, or that the largest double-ended ferries in the United States would be assigned to the route.

Passenger steamers held down the run in the early years, sailing from Eagle Harbor and Eagledale to Seattle. Operated by the Kitsap County Transportation Company, auto ferry service started in 1923 with the rebuilt car ferry *Liberty*, which had started life as the passenger steamer *City of Everett*. The ferry *Bainbridge* took over the run in 1928.

One ferry was enough for the route, augmented by passenger steamer in the summer months. Black Ball officially took over the operation in 1935, but the *Bainbridge* continued on her namesake route. It wasn't until the first of the San Francisco boats arrived that the lineup changed, the *Klahanie* becoming the permanent vessel. By 1941, traffic required two ferries traveling to and from Seattle and Winslow, and the *Klahanie* was paired up with sister *Elwha (I)*.

The *Chippewa* was on the route in June 1951 when Washington State Ferries took over the route, and the story goes she spent half the day with her smokestack painted red on one side and the new Washington State Ferries green on the other while they painted her en route.

With the Agate Pass Bridge opening in 1950 and the more direct route to the north end of the Kitsap Peninsula, traffic grew at a rapid pace. The Wood Electric ferries were no longer large enough to meet demand, and vessels were shuffled to meet the schedule. The Steel Electric Class ferry *Illahee* became a mainstay, and in 1954 the first new ferry built for Washington State Ferries was assigned to the route—the *Evergreen State*. In 1959, the *Illahee* would be paired with the *Tillikum*, an arrangement that would carry on for another eight years, with summer service augmented by the *Chippewa* or *San Mateo*.

By the time the Supers arrived in 1967-68, it was apparent that they weren't going to meet demands on the run. Bainbridge Island's shifting demographic had changed from a rural community with farms and summer cabins to an affordable alternative to living in Seattle. Moreover, as the direct route to downtown, the entire north end of Kitsap County migrated toward the Seattle-Winslow route as the quickest way to reach offices in downtown Seattle.

From 1973-1997, the *Spokane* and *Walla Walla*, then the largest double-ended ferries in the world, would be the primary vessels on the run, replaced with their slightly larger cousins, the Jumbo Mark IIs, arriving in 1997-99.

DEFUNCT ROUTE: SEATTLE-INDIANOLA-SUQUAMISH

Another contributing factor to the Seattle-Winslow run suddenly becoming more heavily traveled was the elimination of the Suquamish-Indianola-Seattle run. The state closed the route when the tolls came off the Agate Pass Bridge in October of 1951, considering it unprofitable. Commuters who had once used this route now shifted to the Winslow run.

EDMONDS-KINGSTON

Today, the Kingston-Edmonds route is served most often by the *Puyallup* and *Spokane*, two of the largest vessels in the fleet that can move a great deal of cars. Even with their capacity, two and sometimes three-hour backups on the popular run are not uncommon during the summer months.

As the adage goes about "location being everything," the short jump between the two cities still grants the most direct route to the wilds of the Olympic Peninsula from the major population centers on the east side of the Sound. From Kingston, a short drive up the highway will put you at the Hood Canal Bridge and not far from Olympic National Park.

Established as the Port Ludlow-Kingston-Edmonds route, two boats were necessary to keep the schedule. With the Port Ludlow portion of the route dropped by 1950, a single vessel was able to hold traffic down between Edmonds and Kingston, with extra service happening during the summer. By the middle of that decade, two boats were needed full-time, with three in the summer months on weekends and holidays. By 1973, traffic had increased enough to make a Super Class ferry necessary, starting with the *Elwha (II)*. Into the 1980s, the *Chelan* and *Yakima* were paired on the route, but a second Super was called for by the early 1990s. *Hyak* and *Yakima* were mostly paired on the run, but back-ups continued as populations on both sides of the water continued to grow. With the addition of the Jumbo Mark IIs starting in 1997, the Jumbo Class first appeared at Kingston. Since that time, the pairing of the *Puyallup* and *Spokane* has been most often the duo shuttling traffic across the water. Plans for this route call for year-round three boat service as soon as new ferries are built.

DEFUNCT ROUTES: EDMONDS-PORT TOWNSEND, PORT LUDLOW-BALLARD, HOOD CANAL, BRINNON-SEABECK, PORT GAMBLE-SHINE, LOFALL-SOUTH POINT

In addition to the Port Ludlow service mentioned above, for many years there had been direct Edmonds to Port Townsend ferry service, not stopping at Kingston. The route was covered by the 33-car *Indianapolis*, perhaps one of the least successful-looking conversions from steamer to car ferry. She was retired and scrapped as soon as the *Chetzemoka (I)* could replace her. The *Chetzemoka (I)* made the last run between the two cities in 1939. The route would be reactivated unexpectedly in 1979 when the Hood Canal Bridge sank. At various times there has been talk of operating a direct link from Port Townsend to Edmonds or Seattle as a passenger-only operation, but so far no one has figured out a way to make the run work economically.

Hood Canal had several routes established on it before World War I, with the steamer *Potlatch* being built specifically for it. It seems Black Ball was never able to turn a profit on it and discontinued service in 1917, selling off the *Potlatch* in the process.

Auto ferry service on Hood Canal was primarily run by Berte Olson. She ran the ferries between Brinnon and Seabeck, and later between Port Gamble on the Kitsap Peninsula and Shine on the Olympic Peninsula. A great friend to Captain Peabody, he actually owned the run while she operated the ferries and sailed some of the vessels.

Olson had started out running across Deception Pass but had been put out of business when the Deception Pass Bridge opened. She moved her vessels over to the Canal and set up shop there, retiring in 1950 when Captain Peabody's Lofall-South Point link was established.

Captain Peabody knew larger ferries were needed to cross the Canal and provide access to the Olympic Peninsula. The Port Gamble-Shine run with its tiny vessels would not be adequate, so he built the docks and roads at Lofall and South Point. Washington State Ferries took over the run with the others in 1951. When the Hood Canal Floating Bridge opened in 1961, the route was discontinued, only to be reactivated again when the bridge sank in 1979. A tug and barge service started between the old docks but was halted abruptly when an accident resulted in the death of a worker when the barge overran the tug. Ferry service was quickly reestablished, and the Lofall-South Point route operated until 1982 when the rebuilt Hood Canal Bridge reopened.

PORT TOWNSEND-KEYSTONE (COUPEVILLE)

Today it's officially called the Port Townsend-Coupeville run, but don't expect to drive off the ferry on Whidbey Island and right into downtown Coupeville—the town actually lies five miles from the ferry dock. The decision to rename the route was a political one, not a practical one.

Ferry service between the Victorian City on the Olympic Peninsula side and Whidbey Island dates back to 1925 when the *Mount Vernon* started the route, summers only. The body of water between the two ports, Admiralty Inlet, is notoriously tetchy, subject to currents, strong tides, thick fogs, and winds that can come out of two directions at once.

Black Ball operated the run with a variety of different ferries over the years—*Beeline*, *Rosario*, *Clatawa*, *Quilcene*, and the *Kitsap*. In 1943, after the season shut down on

October 15, Black Ball never operated the route again. The dock was destroyed in a storm and never rebuilt. They sold the route to Captain Oscar Lee in 1947, and after building a new dock in the man-made harbor at Keystone, ferry service resumed with the *Fox Island* in 1948. Lee upgraded his vessel in 1953 with the *Defiance*, another former Washington Navigation Company vessel, and from then until 1971 the *Defiance* sailed summers only.

Olympic Ferries Inc. purchased the *San Diego* from the San Diego-Coronado Ferry Company to replace the *Defiance*. She sailed for two years before Olympic Ferries shut down for good after the summer season in 1973. Washington State Ferries was ordered to pick up the run, and in June 1974, the *Olympic (II)* established the new state service.

Within a year, service was established year-round, first with the *Olympic (II)* and then the *Rhododendron*. The refurbished *Klickitat* was assigned to the route in 1982, establishing a long career there, staying mainly on the route until ordered out of service in 2007.

The abrupt removal of the Steel Electric Class from service in 2007 resulted in Washington State Ferries chartering the *Steilacoom II* from Pierce County, receiving a special waiver from the Coast Guard to operate the flat-keeled boat across Admiralty Inlet. Initially the state planned to build clones of the *Steilacoom II* for the route. By the time legislators boarded the ferry in Port Townsend to cross to Keystone to see just how the vessel was doing, crews had already nicknamed the boat "Bob" for the way it handled—bobbing across the water even in mild seas.

Upon arrival in Keystone, a group of green-faced legislators decided that "Bob" was not the way to go. New ferries would have to be built more in line with the predecessors. In 2010, the first new "Kwa-di-Tabil" ("little boat" in the Quileute language) class boat, the *Chetzemoka (II),* was in service, with near sisters *Salish* and *Kennewick* following in 2011 and 2012.

MUKILTEO-CLINTON

Last of the Central Sound Routes is the long-established link between Clinton on Whidbey Island and Mukilteo. Like the Port Townsend route, this ferry run underwent a name change. Until 1979, it was the Mukilteo-Columbia Beach run.

A number of small ferries were used on the crossing for the Whidby Island Transportation Company, the largest of which was the *Whidby*. Like so many other companies, eventually they would be bought out by Puget Sound Navigation. By 1928, the run was Black Ball's, operating with the *Puget* and *Washington*.

This second *Washington* should not be confused with the former Lake Washington steam ferry of the same name. This barge-like diesel ferry had been built for use on the Columbia River in 1923 for the Longview Ferry Company. Black Ball purchased it secondhand and used it on the Mukilteo run, primarily as a secondary vessel. Like many other of the older, smaller vessels in the Black Ball Fleet, the *Washington* was retired in 1939 with the arrival of the California ferries.

Over the years, Mukilteo would become known for its long-lasting ferry assignments, particularly with Washington State Ferries. For much of the 1940s, the *Bainbridge* and *Kitsap* were the two most often paired. The *Chetzemoka (I)* would arrive in 1947 and stay there throughout the 50s and much of the 60s, joined by another long-timer, the *Olympic (II)*. *Olympic (II)* would be reunited with sister *Rhododendron* until 1974; with the arrival of the Issaquah Class, the *Cathlamet* would be assigned to the route and stay there until 2016, with sister *Kittitas* joining her after her stint on Hood Canal and where she too has worked for most of her career.

After many years of studies and failed attempts to move the dock from the inadequate ferry landing that has been in the same spot since the days of the *Puget* and *Washington*, Mukilteo is finally getting a new, modern, multimodal ferry terminal. Scheduled to open in 2020, the new terminal will play host to two Olympic Class vessels for the summer months—*Tokitae*, permanently assigned to the route, and *Suquamish*.

We'll see how long this pairing will last.

One of the ferries that started it all—much to the bane of many a West Seattle resident. The steam ferry *Washington* started service at Fauntleroy a century ago after being freed up from duty on Lake Washington. Traffic has steadily grown on the run while the dock and holding area have not, resulting in traffic headaches on the road leading to the terminal. The *Washington* would spend time as an excursion ship before being taken over for the war effort. As a floating machine shop, she lasted until at least the late 1960s before disappearing from the record.

The *Lincoln*, also a former Lake Washington ferry, was used by the residents of Vashon to set up their own ferry company in the wake of PSN's resistance to be taken over by the state. Already in deplorable condition by the late 1940s, it was said that Puget Sound could be seen through the timbers on the car deck. The old veteran was replaced by the much newer and freshly rebuilt *Crosline*. [*Courtesy of the Captain Raymond W Hughes Collection, colorized*]

A very rare photo of the *Crosline* taken before state ownership, dating the photo to sometime between 1947 and 1951. The little vessel seems to have been terminally camera shy, very few post-state ownership photos having been taken of her. She's seen here at the Fauntleroy dock.

The *Quinault*, May 1953. The last of the Steel Electrics to have the large car deck windows changed into portholes, the presence of Navy vessels indicates the photo was taken during the Seattle Maritime Festival.

Two long-timers on the Vashon run. *Klahowya*, built in 1958 and seen from the *Quinault*, worked at Vashon nearly her entire sixty-year career. The *Quinault*, already forty-three years old when this photo was taken in 1970, would sail another thirty-seven years, undergoing a second major rebuild in 1987 before being yanked from service in 2007.

The *Klahowya* approaching Fauntleroy, her gold stripes on her stacks for fifty years of service. The ferry spent the last few years of her long career as the inter-island boat in the San Juan Islands, after working the Vashon Island run from 1958-2014. *[Courtesy of Matt Masuoka]*

Above: Issaquah, first of the Issaquah Class ferries, has been calling at Vashon since the late 1980s. Saddled with a psychotic computer system, the entire class routinely smashed into or pulled away from docks when they were first introduced between 1978-82. The entire class was subject to multiple lawsuits, forced tie-ups by the Coast Guard, and lengthy and expensive rebuilds. Early teething problems aside, the class has been one of the most reliable and fuel efficient in the fleet for over 30 years. *[Courtesy of Matt Masuoka]*

Left: Relic of an earlier boat of the same name, this life ring from the *Kitsap* of 1925 is on board the second vessel of the same name built in 1980. Formerly a Bremerton boat and then a relief, the *Kitsap* is scheduled to be permanently assigned to the Vashon route in spring, 2019. *[Courtesy of Brandon Moser]*

Sealth, last of the Issaquah Class, spent months tied up at Lake Union while WSF and her builder, Marine Power & Equipment, fought in the courts. The only vessel in the series of six not to have been expanded to carry additional cars, the ferry is expected to take over duty in the San Juan Islands as the inter-island vessel in 2019. Her lack of second car decks gives her the advantage of being able to carry over-height vehicles throughout, which is a much-appreciated asset in the Islands. She is seen here on the Vashon route where she has spent the last several years as the number three vessel on the route. *[Courtesy of Matt Masuoka]*

The *Cathlamet* distinguished her early career by demolishing the dock at Mukilteo, and then a week later taking out the dock in Clinton. Victim to the same buggy computer system the entire class had when she debuted in 1981, the problem was fixed with the computer equivalent of a brain transplant. The ferry would spend the next thirty-odd years at Mukilteo before being replaced by the bigger *Tokitae* and reassigned to Vashon Island, where she is pictured here. *[Courtesy of Matt Masuoka]*

THE WILLAMETTE IRON & STEEL WORKS
OF PORTLAND

REQUEST YOUR PRESENCE AT

THE LAUNCHING OF THE

STEAMER H. B. KENNEDY

FOR THE

NAVY YARD ROUTE OF SEATTLE

ON SATURDAY, NOVEMBER 28, 1908

AT THREE P. M.

SHIPYARD IS LOCATED ON FRONT STREET,
BETWEEN 17TH AND 19TH STREETS. TAKE
S CAR ON THIRD STREET, GOING NORTH,
DIRECT TO WORKS, OR 16TH STREET CAR
TO 17TH AND THURMAN, THEN WALK NORTH

Left: The launch of the *H.B. Kennedy* for the Seattle-Bremerton or "Navy Yard Route" was a major event in 1908.

Below: Although the sternwheeler *Bailey Gatzert* had been converted to carry cars, the first proper car ferry was the converted steamer *Whatcom* which emerged as the *City of Bremerton* in 1921. Single-ended ferries became the standard on the Bremerton run, which, despite having to back into the dock at Bremerton, could still be operated faster than the double-ended ferries at that time. *[Colorized]*

Above: Passenger steamers were still needed during the transition between steamer to ferry. Here, the *Tacoma*, no longer needed as the Tacoma-Seattle run had been discontinued, sails into a Rich Passage sunset in 1934. The large lower deck windows would soon be plated in, portholes taking their place, and the crack steamer would be assigned to successful excursion trips to Canada. *[Colorized]*

Right: H.B. *Kennedy* was renamed *Seattle* to complement the *Tacoma* on the Seattle-Tacoma run. She didn't last long in that capacity, as the run was soon discontinued. The *City of Bremerton* soon needed a running mate as customers demanded more accommodation for auto service. In 1924 the *Seattle* was rebuilt as a car ferry, quickly becoming the most popular ferry on the route.

Left: Brass gleaming in the sun, a mother and her son enjoy a crossing on the *Seattle* in the 1920s. *[Colorized]*

Below: The *Seattle* retained many of her attributes from her steamer days, including a luxurious interior and perhaps most importantly to her patrons, her speed. Expanding the vessel had actually resulted in a slight *increase* in speed. The ferry could easily make the crossing in forty-five minutes or slightly under. *[Colorized]*

Long associated with Bremerton route, the 1900-built *Chippewa*, once the source of the rate war with Canadian Pacific on the run from Seattle to Victoria, was idled after spending the First World War as a training platform. For nearly a decade she sat at Lake Union, rusting away, until demand for more auto capacity prompted PSN to rebuild the ferry in 1926.

The rather idealized drawing of the "new" flagship shows the *Chippewa* as she looked after her 1926 rebuild, still sporting many characteristics of her former passenger steamer self. Originally been built for the Great Lakes with a heavier hull than the *Seattle*, sponsoning the ferry to carry cars reduced the *Chippewa*'s top speed. Becoming unprofitable to operate as a steam-powered vessel, six years later the ferry would undergo a second major rebuild.

This color photograph shows just how striking the "Black Ball red" really was. The *Chippewa*, repowered with a Busch-Sulzer diesel, left the yard with a cabin fitted out with Philippine mahogany. Among other amenities were a full-service lunch counter, men's smoking room and ladies' lounge, and the first of Black Ball's "Moonlight Cruises" with live music.

At her final Coast Guard inspection in 1964, the cabin of the *Chippewa* shows itself to still be resplendent in well-cared for mahogany. All the beautiful woodwork would be destroyed by an arsonist in 1968.

The inglorious end to the *Chippewa*. Seen here in Oakland after the fire in June 1968, the vessel was a total loss. Undeterred, Donald Clair, who had purchased the ferry in hopes of creating a maritime museum and floating tourist venue, returned to Puget Sound and picked up another idled ferry—the former Southern Pacific Golden Gate ferry *Santa Rosa*.

Above left: This extremely rare brochure shows how the *Kalakala* was originally designed—a very conventional looking ferry, a larger version of the *Chippewa*. This brochure appeared as late as early 1935, mere months before the debut of soon-to-be world-famous Art Deco streamliner.

Above right: Take two. This is the more well-known brochure, showing the stylized version of the aluminum-painted ferry.

Advertising the Seattle World's Fair in 1962, the by then nearly thirty-year-old *Kalakala* still wowed tourists, becoming the second most popular attraction—behind only the Space Needle.

By 1966, when this photo was taken, the *Kalakala* was showing her age. Lightly constructed in 1935, her cabin needed major renewals, her car deck needed replating, and her gigantic Busch-Sulzer diesel was both expensive to maintain and difficult to find parts for. Her narrow beam, at just 55 feet, made loading late 1960s-sized cars a challenge. The state retired her in 1967. After spending three decades in Alaska, she returned to Puget Sound, but never was able to muster enough financial support for restoration. Increasingly fragile and in danger of sinking, the old streamliner was scrapped in 2015.

Why Wills' Cigarette company felt compelled to include the *Fresno* in their "Strange Craft" series is known only to them. One of six nearly identical ferries, all would leave San Francisco to work on Puget Sound. *Fresno* with sister *Santa Rosa* would be rebuilt especially for the Bremerton run to carry more passengers for the increasing traffic to the Puget Sound Naval Shipyard, already ramping up for the war in 1940. Repowered with Busch-Sulzer diesels, the ferries would emerge as the single-ended ferries *Willapa* and *Enetai*.

The interior of the *Fresno* prior to rebuilding. All six ferries had curved observation rooms at the forward end of each passenger cabin. *[Colorized]*

Willapa in Black Ball livery. The ferries were nearly identical, but after the addition of radar in the late 1940s would become distinguishable. *Willapa*'s radar unit was placed behind the wheelhouse on the crew's quarters; *Enetai*'s was placed on the wheelhouse roof.

Willapa in 1963. By this time WSF was already looking to rid itself of its single-enders. *Chippewa* would go first in 1964, a victim of its low car deck clearance and exorbitant repairs needed for Coast Guard recertification. *Kalakala* and *Willapa* would go next in 1967 with the arrival of the *Hyak*. *Enetai* would last until 1968, idled when the *Yakima* went into service. Neglected for more than four decades, the *Willapa* sank at least once before being hauled up the Sacramento River where she was scrapped on site between 2009-2014.

Lone survivor of the six sisters, *Enetai* would return to San Francisco under her original name, *Santa Rosa*. She remains there today at Pier 3, the headquarters for Hornblower Yachts, available for parties and social gatherings of all types. Her aft wheelhouse has been restored, but she still has the expanded passenger cabin PSN put in place in 1940. She's seen here arriving in Seattle in 1963.

Napa Valley, a former Southern Pacific steamer, joined the fleet in 1942 to add much needed capacity to the Bremerton route. The Puget Sound Naval Shipyard was working twenty-four hours a day by this time, and the rotating shifts were taxing the four ferries on the route. Renamed *Malahat*, an errant cigarette burned up her passenger cabin in March 1943. Rebuilt, she worked the rest of the war on the route. Not included in the sale to the state in 1951, she saw little work after the sale. This scarce color photo shows the awkward looking vessel tied up in West Seattle. Sold in 1956, she was destroyed by fire in Portland later that year.

One of the longest-lived ferries on Puget Sound started life as the *Asbury Park* in 1901. As an auto-carrier on San Francisco Bay, she was renamed *City of Sacramento*. Added to the Puget Sound fleet in 1944, she became the *sixth* ferry on the Bremerton run. Idled after the war, Captain Peabody took the old steamer to Canada, stripped her to the hull and rebuilt her as the *Kahloke* in 1953. She would sail for him until Black Ball was bought out by British Columbia Ferries; as *Langdale Queen* she would continue to work until 1976. Sold, sunk, raised, and stripped down to a barge, the hull would continue working until sinking again in 2008. *[Colorized]*

Nearing the end of her career as a ferry, the *Langdale Queen*, ex-*Kahloke*, ex-*City of Sacramento*, ex-*Asbury Park* looked particularly lovely after her final rebuild and in the pastel blue livery of B.C. Ferries.

The Black Ball Fleet of 1945.
Astonishingly, ten of these vessels
(in varying conditions) would
survive into the twenty-first
century.

Langdale Queen, which had been renamed *Lady Grace* after being sold by B.C. Ferries, sunk at her berth. The mudline is well in evidence here in this photo. The time underwater would have disastrous consequences on her upperworks, which deteriorated rapidly and resulted in her being stripped down to the hull for conversion to a barge. *[Courtesy of the Byrne Family Collection]*

The *Tyee* was the first passenger-only ferry for WSF. The program would expand in fits and starts before finally being abandoned for its high operation costs.

The *Skagit* and *Kalama* were two of the most unpopular vessels to every sail for WSF. Cramped and uncomfortable, the two handled rough seas poorly, and proved to be unreliable. Sold to a boat broker who then passed them on to a ferry company in Tanzania, the *Skagit*, dangerously overloaded, capsized in rough weather sailing to Zanzibar. Well over a hundred passengers were lost. The *Kalama* was removed from service by Tanzanian authorities, and her current whereabouts are unknown.

The *Chinook* and *Snohomish* were two passenger-only fast ferries (POFF) boats that could make the crossing to Bremerton in as little as a half an hour. Traveling at high speed, their wake did not have sufficient time to flatten out in narrow Rich Passage, resulting in erosion of the beaches. Forced to slow down in the passage, the high-speed advantage was lost, and the ferries were mothballed. *[Courtesy of Matt Masuoka]*

Both of the POFF ferries would go on to prosperous second lives. Now operating in San Francisco as *Napa* and *Golden Gate,* the ferries have worked out very well for their new owners. *[Courtesy of Brandon Moser]*

The *Hyak*'s career has come full circle. Starting on the Bremerton run, she moved from the route in the late 70s to spend time at Kingston and the San Juans before returning back to the Bremerton route. The only Super Class ferry not to have undergone a mid-life refit, she looks almost the same now as she did when she first arrived from San Diego in June 1967. Sporting her fifty-year service stripes, the ferry is due to be retired in 2019. *[Courtesy of Matt Masuoka]*

The Super Class ferries *Yakima* and *Kaleetan* in 1968. The *Yakima* worked alongside the *Hyak* on the Bremerton while the *Kaleetan* and *Elwha* held down traffic between Seattle and Winslow. The ferries were identical in every way—so much so that after several people ended up in Bremerton when actually wanting to go to Winslow and vice versa—WSF placed nameboards under the wheelhouse windows so passengers could tell the vessels apart. The idea stuck, and all ferries have nameboards under the wheelhouses to this day. Off to the right, the Matson ocean liner *Mariposa* or *Monterey* can be seen.

A view of the *Kaleetan's* twin stacks, sporting their fifty-year service stripes. After leaving the Seattle-Winslow route, she spent the next twenty-five years in the San Juan Islands. Rebuilt in the late 1990s, she's since become one of the primary vessels on the Bremerton run.

The colors of autumn fall softly on the *Kaleetan* as she arrives from Bremerton in October 2018. *[Courtesy of Matt Masuoka]*

A far cry from the tiny *City of Bremerton*, the *Chimacum* joined the Bremerton route in 2017. This ferry and her sisters in the Olympic Class appear to be the ideal size for most of the central Puget Sound routes, and are planned to replace many of the older boats in the years to come. *[Courtesy of Matt Masuoka]*

The *Bainbridge*, built in 1928, was one of the first auto ferries to serve its island namesake for the Kitsap County Transportation Company or "White Collar Line," so dubbed due to the white band on the smokestacks. Under PSN, the ferry moved around Puget Sound a great deal. Captain Peabody took the ferry to Canada, where she is seen here arriving at Horseshoe Bay in the 1950s.

The *Kehloken* would arrive in 1938 and become a "Bainbridge boat." The ferry had the unhappy task of transporting the island's Japanese-Americans to Seattle for relocation to internment camps during WWII. Leading an otherwise uneventful life, after retirement she was destroyed by a spectacular fire while moored on Lake Washington in 1979. The hulk was later towed out to Possession Point off Whidbey Island and turned into an artificial reef. *[Colorized]*

Kehloken, tied up and undergoing maintenance. Perhaps sensing the end of his operations, Captain Peabody hadn't put a lot of effort into keeping the fleet up in the late 1940s. While generally shipshape, each vessel had a backlog of maintenance upon transfer to the state. The early years of WSF were spent reconditioning each vessel, which included a very liberal use of the new Washington State Ferries green. *[Courtesy of Belvedere-Tiburon Landmarks Society, colorized]*

The first *Elwha* ran opposite the *Kehloken* for several years. For reasons lost to history, PSN decided they could live without the *Elwha* and sold her to the San Diego-Coronado Ferry Company where she would sail as the *Silver Strand*. *[Colorized]*

Right: Far from the fogs and steady rain of the Pacific Northwest, the former *Elwha* enjoyed a long career at San Diego. The *Silver Strand* lasted until the Coronado bridge retired her. She ended up a wreck on the Los Angeles breakwater after being demolished by a storm on November 30, 1970.

Below: The beloved *Illahee*, formerly the *Lake Tahoe*, became a "Bainbridge Boat" throughout the 50s and 60s. Built in 1927, she spent over sixty years on Puget Sound, becoming a familiar sight to generations of commuters and tourists.

Above: An ignominious end after eighty years of service, the *Illahee* sank and capsized while at the scrapping basin in Ensenada, Mexico. *[Courtesy of Shawn J. Dake]*

Left: Food on the ferries has varied a great deal over the years. For decades, meals were cooked on board and made to order. This menu dates from the WSF era (hence the green) and once was onboard the *Klahanie.*

Fruits and Juices

Orange Juice, fresh	.15
Orange Juice, canned	.10
Grapefruit Juice	.10
Pineapple Juice	.10
Tomato Juice	.10
Sliced Orange	.10
Grapefruit, Peaches, Prunes	.10
Fresh Fruits in Season	.15

Cereals

Dry Cereal with Cream	.15
Hot Cereal with Cream	.15

Toast, Rolls, Etc.

Toast, (2 slices) with Jelly	.10
Toast, (3 slices) Dry or Buttered	.10
Cinnamon Toast	.20
Milk Toast	.20
French Toast with Syrup, Jelly, or Honey	.35
Doughnuts (3)	.10
Small Pastries	.05
with Butter	.10
Butterhorn (with Butter)	.15
Side Order Jelly	.10
Extra Butter	.05

Breakfast Specials

Hotcakes & Coffee	.25
Two Eggs, Fried, Boiled or Scrambled, with Toast and Coffee	.30

Three Eggs, Fried, Boiled or Scrambled, with Toast and Coffee	.40
One Egg with 3 slices Bacon, or Sausage, Toast and Coffee	.35
Plain Omelette with Toast and Coffee	.35
Omelette with Cheese, Ham, Bacon, or Jelly, Toast and Coffee	.45
Side Order Eggs (1)	.10
Side Order Eggs (2)	.15
Side Order Bacon (3 slices)	.15
Side Order Ham	.20
Breakfast Bacon, (4 slices), Toast and Coffee	.30
Grilled Ham, Toast and Coffee	.35
Side Order Hashed Brown Potatoes with Above Orders	.10
2 Eggs, Potatoes, Toast and Coffee	.35
Bacon and Eggs, Potatoes, Toast and Coffee	.50
Ham and Eggs, Potatoes, Toast and Coffee	.50

Sandwiches

Peanut Butter	.15
Peanut Butter Jelly	.15
Boiled Ham	.15
Minced Ham & Pickle	.15
Cheese	.15
Tunafish	.15
Liverwurst	.15
Egg Salad	.15

Fried Egg	.15
Hamburger with Relish or Onions	.15
Hamburger with Lettuce and Tomato	.20
Hamburger with Cheese	.20
Lettuce and Tomato	.20
Ham and Cheese	.20
Fried Ham or Bacon	.20
Toasted Cheese	.20
Sardine	.20
Cold Roast Meat	.20
Ham and Egg	.25
Bacon and Egg	.25
Bacon and Tomato	.25
Chicken Salad	.25
Sliced Chicken	.40
Club House	.40
Hot Roast Meat with Potatoes and Gravy	.35

Salads to Order

Steaks

(Includes Coffee)

Hamburger Steak	.40
(with Onions)	.45
Cubed Steak	.50
Club Steak	.60
Sirloin Steak	.75
T-Bone Steak	.85

Desserts

	.0
Pie or Cake	.10
a la Mode	.15
Doughnuts (3)	.10
Small Pastries	.05
with Butter	.10
Butterhorn (with Butter)	.15
Pudding or Jell-O	.10

Hot and Cold Drinks

Coffee	.05
Milk	.05
Hot Chocolate	.10
Tea, Black or Green	.10
Western Beer	.15
Eastern Beer	.20

Fountain Menu

Fountain Drinks	.05
Ice Cream, Dish	.10
Sundaes	.15
Ice Cream Sodas	.15
Milk Shake	.15
Malted Milk	.20
Egg Malted Milk	.25
Alka Seltzer	.10
Bromo Seltzer	.10
7-Up, Pints	.25
Gingerale, Pints	.25
White Rock, Bottle	.25

Prices have changed just a little over the years. It appears the most expensive item is the T-bone steak at 85 cents.

Black Ball never utilized the *Shasta*, seen here, or her sister *San Mateo* much. WSF would change that, using the steamers for extra summer service at Vashon, Kingston, and Bainbridge. The *Shasta* had a bad habit of smoking profusely. WSF sold the *Shasta* in 1958.

Renamed the *Centennial Queen*, the former *Shasta* sailed up and down the Columbia River for Oregon's centennial celebrations in 1959. The ferry did *not* ditch her habit of belching huge plumes of oily black smoke, as is evident in this photograph. Even after achieving some height, the smoke is doing a fairly good job of blotting out Mount Hood.

Turned into a floating restaurant and renamed the "River Queen," the 1922-built steamer enjoyed a long and successful career right up until she lost her moorage in 1995. Unable to find a permanent home, the vessel changed hands several times until she ended up moored at Goble, Oregon and falling into further disrepair. Deemed a hazard, the Coast Guard seized the vessel and began scrapping her in the summer of 2018.

The *San Mateo* would also become a much beloved boat. Her cabin featured carved posts and stained-glass clerestory windows, harkening back to the elegance of a bygone era. Pictured here doing extra service on the Seattle-Winslow route, the *San Mateo* became the last steam-powered ferry on the west coast, retiring on Labor Day, 1969.

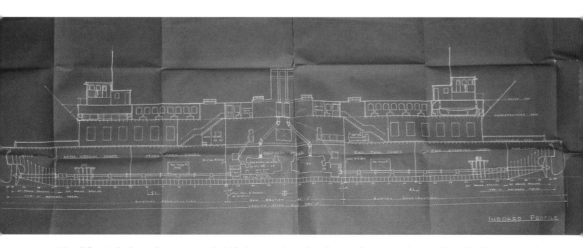

Her life might have been extended if plans to lengthen her and convert her to diesel had transpired. The blueprints show just how altered the steamer would have been. For better or worse, the plan never came to anything. *[Courtesy of Byrne Family Collection]*

Left: Hailed as the solution to all the capacity woes on the Seattle-Winslow route, the Super Class ferries were already outpaced by traffic by 1970. Two new ferries were built, dubbed the "Jumbo Class." Together, the *Walla Walla* and *Spokane* would appear in hundreds of postcards and countless WSF brochures from their introduction in 1973 until they were displaced by their larger cousins in 1997-98.

Below: The only thing the *Tacoma* has in common with her namesake predecessor is her speed, which although she has never had to travel at it, was well over 20 knots during trials. The largest double-ended ferries in the United States, the class is scheduled to undergo a conversion to hybrid-electric propulsion. *[Courtesy of Matt Masuoka]*

Above: The Jumbo Mark II Class ferries *Tacoma, Wenatchee* and *Puyallup* are modern icons of Puget Sound. With either the snow-covered Olympic Mountains or the picturesque skyline of Seattle as a backdrop, along with spectacular views in any direction, it is easy to see why the ferries are the number one tourist draw in Washington State. *[Courtesy of Matt Masuoka]*

Right: Sound Ferry Lines lasted a very short time before being bought out by PSN. The Edmonds-Kingston route, which had been established with tiny ten-car ferries, received its first "big boat" with the *Quillayute* in 1927.

EDMONDS
OLYMPIC *Route*

The New and Palatial Auto-Passenger Ferry "QUILLAYUTE"—Capacity 60 Cars

Direct Route to the Olympic Peninsula
Port Angeles, Port Townsend, Lake Crescent, Mora-on-the-Pacific

IF YOU want to get the most out of life for yourself and family *this* summer discover the Olympic Peninsula. No discovery you could make offers greater returns in health and happiness. Nothing else you could do can repay you so in pleasure and invigoration.

And best of all its discovery is neither expensive nor difficult, for this great out-of-doors is just across the street from Seattle—just a few miles away by convenient automobile ferry service or splendid highways. A couple of hours and you are in the midst of an incomparable summerland—majestic, snow-capped mountains, sapphire lakes, beautiful, sparkling streams, giant evergreen forests, Alpine parks and mammoth glaciers. Everywhere natural beauties and wonders beckon your attention; everywhere rest, relaxation, happiness and invigoration await you. Splendid highways lead the way and hospitable resorts and picturesque camping sites bid you linger and rest.

Not only does the Olympic Peninsula afford delightful possibilities for summer vacations, but its convenience and ease of access make it particularly attractive as a week-end playground. So great is the variety of its attractions and recreational opportunities that you may spend every week-end during the summer in this glorious out-of-doors and no two in the same way or place. So easy is it of access that little of your time is spent going and returning, but the major part of it in sheer enjoyment.

Slip over and discover this Paradise Peninsula *this* week-end and forever answer the perplexing question: "Where shall we spend this week-end, or vacation?"

SOUND FERRY LINES *Inc.*

Built in 1927, the all-wood *Quillayute* was not included in the sale of PSN to Washington State. She would sail in British Columbia for Black Ball and B.C. Ferries for a time before being converted into a floating fish camp renamed *Samson IV*. Remarkably, the ferry lasted until 2003 when Canadian officials discovered that, despite her hull being stuffed with foam plastic, the old ferry was in danger of sinking. To head off an environmental catastrophe, the *Quillayute* was towed to shore and broken up.

The former *Mendocino*, renamed *Nisqually* (seen here in 1962), spent many years on the Kingston run, becoming the main vessel on the route through the 50s and 60s. The Steel Electrics became such an iconic symbol for WSF that their profile still appears as the system logo, a decade after their removal from Puget Sound.

Right: The *Nisqually* suffered from one of the most serious accidents in WSF history when she collided with the freighter *Taichung* in July 1963. The two hit in thick fog just after the ferry left Kingston. The whistles of the freighter alerted passengers in the galley to take evasive action, which they did just as the vessel smashed into the ferry. Amazingly, no one was hurt. The *Nisqually* carried scars from the accident the rest of her life. *[Courtesy of Byrne Family Collection]*

Below: The Kingston dock in the early 60s, the *Klahanie* at the tie-up slip. Once held down by one or two small vessels, with extra service vessels such as the all-wood *Klahanie* on the weekends, the Kingston-Edmonds route now boasts two of the largest vessels in the fleet and in summer months can routinely have backups of ninety minutes or more.

The *Spokane* moved to the Kingston run with the arrival of cousin ferry *Wenatchee* in 1998. The 1972-built vessel's profile has been the subject of hundreds of postcards, the Philip Spaulding-designed ferry being particularly photogenic. *[Courtesy of Matt Masuoka]*

In the twilight of their service, the Steel Electrics would occasionally fill in as a third boat on the Edmonds-Kingston run. Here the *Quinault* greets her fleet-mate *Walla Walla* at mid-crossing. *[Courtesy of Matt Masuoka]*

Puyallup, third and last of the Jumbo Mark II class, arrived in 1999. Almost always on the Kingston-Edmonds route, the ferry will move to the Seattle-Bainbridge run while the *Tacoma* or *Wenatchee* goes in for maintenance. Rated at 2000 passengers (compared to the Mark II's 2500), the smaller Jumbos' capacity is no longer sufficient for the commuter runs between Seattle and Bainbridge Island, necessitating the *Puyallup* to pinch-hit for one of her sisters. *[Courtesy of Matt Masuoka]*

Walla Walla, once a staple of the Bainbridge run, spends most of her time filling in for the *Spokane* or *Puyallup* for maintenance cycles on the Kingston route. Summers often see the ferry at Bremerton.

Left: The spelling of "Whidbey" has wobbled over the years, far into the 20th century. Many items of Black Ball ephemera have it spelled "Whidby" without the "e." Whidby Island Ferry Lines started out as an independent company, but soon was absorbed by PSN, as is evident by the MAin 2222 phone number on this brochure, which was the PSN number at Colman Dock.

Below: The *Washington* was a harbinger for things to come on the Mukilteo-Clinton route. Not to be confused with the steam-powered former Lake Washington ferry of the same name, this *Washington* had been purchased by PSN secondhand from the Columbia River. A particularly unattractive vessel, the open-deck *Washington* was only ever used on the Mukilteo run and was pulled from service around 1940. *[Courtesy Captain Raymond W. Hughes Collection, colorized]*

Above: The first *Kitsap* had served her namesake county all through her years with the Kitsap County Transportation Company. PSN was not as rigid in their vessel assignments; the *Kitsap* became the first large ferry to serve the Mukilteo-Clinton run. Sold in 1962, she is seen here working her last job on the Astoria-Megler run for the State of Oregon. *[Courtesy Captain Raymond W. Hughes Collection, colorized]*

Right: The *Leschi* was a Lake Washington ferry put out of work by the Mercer Island floating bridge. Formerly a paddlewheel vessel, the conversion to diesel and alterations to her hull made the Coast Guard deem her unsuitable for the longer runs on open stretches of water once she moved to Puget Sound. Used mainly as a back-up boat, she sailed from Mukilteo for a number of years.

PASSENGER
and
AUTO FERRIES

ROUTES, SCHEDULES
and
INFORMATION

LAKE WASHINGTON FERRIES

CAPACITY EACH
50 CARS and 1,000 PASSENGERS

J. L. ANDERSON, Operator
Leschi Park - Seattle, Wn.
Phone EAst 5100

Leschi's outside staircase made her profile unmistakable. The ferry's car capacity dwindling with each passing year, she was finally sold by WSF in 1967. She ended up wrecked in Alaska, where her remains can still be seen today on the beach at Shotgun Cove near Whittier. *[Courtesy of Doug Worthington]*

A rare color photograph of the *Governor Harry W. Nice*, sailing for her original owners. Upon arrival at Puget Sound she would become the second *Olympic* on Puget Sound, spending many years on the Mukilteo-Clinton run.

A passenger stands on deck of the *Olympic* in the 1950s, her red purse a nice contrast to the green and white of the ferry. *Olympic* would remain on the Mukilteo-Clinton route almost exclusively until being moved to the Port Townsend-Keystone run in June 1974.

The first *Chetzemoka*, built in 1927 as the *Golden Poppy* for the Golden Gate ferry company, spent much of her career as running mate to the *Olympic* and *Rhododendron*. By the time this photo was taken, she was used mostly for weekend service. *[Harre Demoro photo, author's collection]*

Nearly identical to the *Chetzemoka*, the large windows on the *Klahanie* were boarded over with sheets of plywood with portholes cut in them to distinguish the ferry from her sister. Over the years the maintenance on these plywood panels fell by the wayside, leading to a somewhat bizarre situation where one side had portholes and one didn't. The ferry is seen here in extra service capacity on the Mukilteo-Clinton run.

A modern version of the earlier open-deck *Washington*, the *Crown City* was built in 1954 for the sunny San Diego-Coronado route. Put out of work by the bridge, WSF snapped up the ferry in 1969 and put her to work on the Mukilteo-Clinton run.

Renamed *Kulshan* and with no galley or real passenger cabin, the ferry quickly became unpopular. Even in the most flattering light, as this photo from 1977 illustrates, the vessel was less than picturesque. In addition, she was a heavy roller in rough seas. Sold in 1982 to the Coast Guard and then again in the 1990s to the Martha's Vineyard Steamship Authority, she is still in service at the Vineyard today as the *Governor*.

The *Rhododendron* first served on Hood Canal before settling in at Mukilteo as the Number One boat. This photo from the 1970s shows her departing Mukilteo for what was then called Columbia Beach (renamed Clinton) with a full load of cars and passengers.

Kittitas is the only Issaquah Class ferry that escaped major issues. She was assigned to the Mukilteo-Clinton route after closing out service on Hood Canal when the bridge reopened and with little variation has been there ever since. In 2018 she made a rare appearance in Friday Harbor as the inter-island vessel, pictured here. *[Photo courtesy of Brandon Moser]*

Tokitae was the first of the Olympic Class ferries built. Seen here on sea trials, the ferry was assigned to the Mukilteo-Clinton route, replacing the *Cathlamet* which had been on the run since first appearing in 1981. Carrying more cars than any other route, the Mukilteo run welcomed the additional capacity.

Suquamish, fourth Olympic Class, joined the fleet in 2018 and will work the Mukilteo during the busy summer months, serving as a relief vessel for the other Olympic Class and Super Class ferries during the rest of the year. This photo was taken while the ferry was on sea trials in a miasma of wildfire smoke that settled over the entire Puget Sound region in the summer of 2018.

Abandoned by PSN in 1943, the Port Townsend-Keystone (now Port Townsend-Coupeville) run was reestablished after WWII at the behest of the military to provide access to bases on either side of the route. Run seasonally by Olympic Ferries Inc, service was started in 1947 with the tiny *Fox Island*. Formerly the *Wollochet*, the ferry was sold to Canadian interests and became the *George S. Pearson*. [*Courtesy Captain Raymond W. Hughes Collection, colorized*]

The M/V *Defiance* sailed the run from 1953 to 1970. The diesel-powered vessel had a steam whistle, which would echo melodiously over the Keystone landing.

The *San Diego*, formerly of the San Diego-Coronado Ferry Company, was already out of service when this photo was taken of her in Canada in the 1980s. Picked up by Olympic Ferries, she ran only from 1971-73. The company went out of business in the fall of 1973, Washington State Ferries resuming service in the summer of 1974 with the *Olympic (II)*.

The *San Diego*, seen here in 1989, was to be rebuilt as a mock sternwheeler in Canada. Renamed *Klondike Queen*, the venture never came to fruition. She eventually made her way back to California, opening as a restaurant in Antioch for a time before being damaged by fire. Plans were made to return her to her namesake city but fell through. Abandoned on the Sacramento River for over a decade, she was scrapped in 2011.

The *Rhododendron*, seen here at Keystone in 1979, worked the Port Townsend-Keystone route with the *Olympic* from the late 70s to the early 1980s. By 1982 the Coast Guard wasn't comfortable with either of the former Baltimore boats working the route. The *Rhody* would see little service from 1983 until her rebuilding in 1991.

Formerly the *Stockton*, the 1927-built *Klickitat* was assigned to the run in 1982 after her final rebuild. She would remain there until 2007. *[Courtesy of Brandon Moser]*

The *Klickitat* arriving at Keystone. This photo illustrates just how narrow Keystone Harbor is, and why sailings must be canceled for tidal conditions several times a year, as the man-made harbor basically empties out. Close enough to shore to hit with a tossed rock (please don't do this), a hefty gust of wind or mechanical failure can result in the ferry landing on the beach instead. Over the years this has happened with every vessel that has worked the route. *[Courtesy of Brandon Moser]*

Salish, second of the "Kwa di Tabil Class" vessels, was originally slated to be a relief inter-island boat in the San Juan Islands in the off season. The ferry's narrow beam, scarcely larger than that of the *Kalakala* built nearly eighty years earlier, has proven to be nearly unworkable for multi-destination loading. After two attempts, the ferry has not been used on the inter-island route since, working as a relief for the *Kennewick* and *Chetzemoka* during maintenance cycles. *[Courtesy of Brandon Moser]*

Last of the class, the *Kennewick* is the year-round resident on the Port Townsend route. Far more suited to the route than "Bob" had been, the volatile conditions on the route—which can change on a dime—still lead to cancellations, most often due to high winds and heavy seas. The ferries can generally handle such conditions, but it can make landing safely at Keystone all but impossible. *[Courtesy of Matt Masuoka]*

BALLARD-LUDLOW

Golden Anchors

Above: The *Ballard* had a second life as a floating restaurant. First called the "Golden Anchors," she was moored on Lake Washington. Later she moved to Lake Union, still an upscale eatery, but later she became a kitschy establishment complete with a giant plastic pirate leering from the smokestack. She would sink twice at Lake Union, the second time finishing her off.

Left: One of the first central Sound routes to be dropped, the Ballard-Port Ludlow route declined in popularity not only because of its length, but the dwindling fortunes of Port Ludlow after the mill shut down. The *Ballard*, like most other vessels on Puget Sound, would end up in the hands of the Puget Sound Navigation Company.

Below: A lonely-looking *Illahee* is en route from Suquamish in the 1940s on wind-swept seas. Abandoned by WSF in 1951, a dock in Suquamish these days would go a long way to alleviate congested traffic across Bainbridge Island, which is restricted to a two-lane highway across the entire length of the Island.

Indianapolis had been hastily converted to carry cars on the Edmonds-Port Townsend-Port Ludlow run. Looking rather awkward with her bow shorn off, the abandonment of the run ended her career. *[Colorized]*

Scrapping the *Indianapolis*. Black Ball scrapped all but a few of its steamers between 1937-39. The *Indianapolis* is about half gone in this photo. Next to her, also being dismantled, is the steamer *Kulshan*.

The trim little steamer *Potlatch* had one of the shortest careers for PSN. Built for Hood Canal service, the company abruptly dropped all of its Hood Canal passenger service in 1917. The *Potlach*, only five years old, seldom saw service again.

The end of the steamer came in 1937. The snapshot shows the *Potlach* stripped down to the hull on the beach.

The *Quillayute* in a rare shot of her at Port Ludlow. The Port Ludlow portion of the Edmonds-Kingston-Port Ludlow route would last until 1950, by which time the once prosperous town had all but been abandoned. *[Colorized]*

The first *Kitsap* spent much of the 1950s as an extra service boat on Hood Canal. Auto service had reverted to PSN when Berte Olson retired, closing the run between Port Gamble and Shine. Captain Peabody moved the route south between Lofall and South Point, where it operated for PSN and WSF until the Hood Canal Floating Bridge opened in 1961. The *Kitsap* is docked at Lofall, taken from the deck of the *Rhododendron*. *[Colorized]*

3

NORTH PUGET SOUND

ANACORTES-SAN JUAN ISLANDS, ANACORTES-GUEMES ISLAND, GOOSEBERRY POINT (BELLINGHAM)-LUMMI ISLAND

The north part of Puget Sound is arguably one of the most beautiful places on earth. From the tulip-filled Skagit Valley to the breathtaking vista of snow-clad Mount Baker, to the sparkling waters and tree-lined shores of the San Juan Islands, the northern ferry routes on the Sound do not lack for scenery.

The ferry routes that exist today are largely unchanged from when steamers first plied the waters. The well-established pattern of smaller companies eventually getting absorbed by Puget Sound Navigation played out in the islands as well. Today, Washington State Ferries handles the major traffic to the San Juan Islands while two county operations remain in service—Skagit County runs the ferry from the city of Anacortes to Guemes Island, and Whatcom County runs the route between Lummi Island and Gooseberry Point near Bellingham.

ANACORTES-SAN JUAN ISLANDS

In the heavy tourist season in the San Juan Islands, five ferries handle traffic on the route. One vessel sails inter-island only, three handle domestic traffic from the mainland, and one makes the forty-mile trek to Sidney, British Columbia twice a day. Not long ago, however, one ferry was all that was needed, including the summer trip to Sidney.

The main difference in traveling the San Juan Islands today from those single-ferry days is the departure point. Washington State Ferries moved the terminal from downtown Anacortes to Ship Harbor in 1960. The large holding area was needed to contain the traffic, which often backed up into downtown Anacortes. The old dock location remains in service today as the ferry terminal for the ferry to Guemes Island.

The major stops in the San Juans also remain the same: Friday Harbor on San Juan Island, Lopez Island, Shaw Island, and Orcas Island. Known for its long waits and miles-long backups on Independence Day, the run today is managed well by a reservation system which has all but eliminated backups. A certain percentage of spaces on the ferries are kept free for drive-ups, but if you want to make your passage as smooth as possible, reserve your spot.

Another notable difference in traveling the San Juan Islands happens in the fall and winter months. Due to the natural topography and unique atmospheric conditions, the north part of Puget Sound can have howling winds when just a few tens of miles south there may be barely a breath of air moving. The Strait of Juan de Fuca also can act like the barrel of a cannon, funneling winds down the water path and raising heavy swells. Waves higher than ten feet are not uncommon during these gales, and at times crossing Rosario Strait which lies just off the Anacortes dock can be a somewhat harrowing experience, particularly if the wind is going against the tide.

Auto ferry service first arrived in the 1920s. Prior to World War I, there were few roads and fewer people to drive them. Steamers like the *Rosalie* transported goods and people to and from ports. After the war, as with everywhere else, the automobile rapidly became the primary mode of transportation. Black Ball responded by rebuilding the *City of Angeles* to carry cars, first installed with the Barlow steam elevator for lifting cars to the docks. By the end of the decade, more modern vessels were added to the run, and throughout the 1930s either the *Quilcene* or *Rosario* managed all traffic in the islands.

By the summer of 1939, two vessels were needed to carry people and cars around, as noted on the schedule which shows that the ferries *Bainbridge* and *Crosline* were assigned to the route. Not surprisingly, during the years of WWII, with travel restricted and gas rationed, only one ferry was needed, this time the *Vashon*. Two-vessel service would resume in 1945 when the *Vashon* would be joined by the *Quillayute*. By the summer of 1950, two Steel Electrics, the *Nisqually* and *Klickitat*, were required to keep up with traffic.

With state ownership, service on the route continued to grow, and some vessels would remain in the islands for years to come. The *Evergreen State* would leave the Bainbridge run in the mid-1950s and after 1959 stay in the San Juan Islands almost exclusively until her retirement from the islands in 2014. The *Vashon* and *Klickitat* would also be assigned to the islands for years.

Traffic increased in the islands to such a degree that by the early 1970s WSF would place the then-largest vessel in the fleet on the run in the spring and summer of 1973: the M/V *Walla Walla*. The Jumbo Class ferry proved to be something less than a success, with complaints about her wake and the vast number of cars being unloaded at one time in Friday Harbor. In addition, some commuters in Seattle, so the story goes, wanted to know why the ferry, partially built with federal mass transit funds, was out in the San Juan Islands, which couldn't be considered a "mass transit hub" by any stretch of the imagination. Not surprisingly, the *Walla Walla* only lasted a single season in the Islands, moving to the Bainbridge Island run and displacing the *Kaleetan*. The *Kaleetan* would move up to the San Juans and spend the next twenty-five years sailing the tree-lined passages and inlets between islands.

While often getting larger, newer vessels, the San Juan Island route hadn't actually had a brand-new vessel assigned to the run since the *Walla Walla* made her dubious debut in the summer of 1973. That changed in 2015 when the brand-new Olympic Class ferry *Samish*, named for the local tribe, started service. The Olympic Class ferry has been such a noted success in the islands it is hoped that more will soon be built to replace the aging Super Class.

ANACORTES-GUEMES ISLAND

This short route has almost always had a ferry named *Guemes* serving it and is notable for the longevity of the vessels on the route.

The first *Guemes* was a wooden, six-car vessel built in 1917. The little ferry transported people to Guemes Island for an astonishing forty-three years, being replaced by the small, steel-hulled ferry *Almar* in 1960. *Almar* lasted until 1979, when she was retired by the current vessel, also named *Guemes*. The 1947-built *Almar* is allegedly still afloat in Alaska, but the Coast Guard has no record for her.

The current *Guemes* is scheduled to be retired soon. Skagit County is looking to replace her with an electric-powered vessel.

LUMMI ISLAND-GOOSEBERRY POINT (BELLINGHAM)

Ferry service to Lummi Island started about the same time as it did on Guemes Island, with the county taking over operations in 1924 with the six-car ferry *Central*. The *Central*, steam-powered and built in 1919, was replaced in 1929 by the *Chief Kwina*. This vessel, augmented by others including the *Pioneer* and *Acorn* over the years, stayed on the route until the *Whatcom Chief* arrived in 1962.

The *Whatcom Chief* is still on the Lummi Island route as of 2019, though Whatcom County is looking into replacement options as of this writing.

DEFUNCT ROUTES: SEATTLE-BELLINGHAM, BELLINGHAM-ORCAS ISLAND, GOOSEBERRY POINT-ORCAS ISLAND, BELLINGHAM-SIDNEY, BRITISH COLUMBIA

Probably the most notable route abandoned by Puget Sound Navigation in the wake of the ferryboat taking over from passenger steamers was the Bellingham-Seattle route. With stops at Anacortes and Everett, the passenger steamer *Kulshan* was the primary vessel on the run from the time of her completion in 1910. *Sol Duc* took over the run in 1929, idling the *Kulshan*, which was not considered for conversion to an auto-carrying vessel. She spent her last years in lay-up, and was finally scrapped in 1938.

Sol Duc maintained the direct link to Seattle from Bellingham until 1935, when transporting freight by diesel truck became cheaper than by aging steamer. Black Ball dropped the run, the *Sol Duc* becoming a barracks ship during WWII, finally being scrapped after the war.

BELLINGHAM-ORCAS ISLAND

The Chuckanut Inter-Island Ferry Company started operations with the *Mount Vernon*, running the ferry from Chuckanut Bay just south of Bellingham to the north end of Orcas Island. Later they chartered the ferry *Rosario*, but couldn't make a financial success of it. The company went bankrupt and the service was dropped by 1940.

GOOSEBERRY POINT-ORCAS ISLAND

A similar run to the Chuckanut Bay-Orcas Island run was held down by the *Mount Vernon* and later the *Chief Kwina* sailing from Gooseberry Point to the same dock at Orcas (near present-day Terrill Beach Road). This service ran for about five years, listed as "temporarily discontinued" in the winter 1935 sailing schedule. Black Ball evidently thought their resources were better used elsewhere and service never resumed.

BELLINGHAM-SIDNEY

An attempt to compete with Black Ball service, the route was started by Canadian Pacific with the first purpose-built diesel ferry—the *Motor Princess*. While the vessel would go on to have a lengthy career, the Bellingham-Sidney run did not, lasting just three years before Canadian Pacific reassigned the *Motor Princess* to the Nanaimo-Vancouver run.

Rosario, rebuilt from the steam ferry *Whidby,* became one of the first proper car ferries in the San Juan Islands. Passengers could spend time observing the stunning scenery from the men's smoking lounge, the forward observation room or the full-service dining room, where tables were set with silverware and linen table cloths. *[Colorized]*

The earliest color slide in the author's collection is this one of the *Rosario*, taken in 1938. The ferries have changed in the San Juan Islands, but the breathtaking views have not.

A useful, if inglorious, end for the *Rosario*. Beached on the banks of the Snohomish River, she became a fish processing plant. This photo, taken in 1971, shows that her appearance didn't change all that much from when she was retired in 1951. She was later plowed under and the hull buried under a parking lot in the 1980s. *[Courtesy of Ken Bhear]*

The crack steamer *Kitsap II* had been totally redesigned once, emerging as the steam ferry *City of Bellingham*. Rebuilt again, she became the *Quilcene*, and served the San Juan Islands for years before being sold in 1940. Seen here zipping through Pole Pass, the ferry could still travel at a good clip. *[Colorized]*

As the *Quilcene*, used on the Anacortes-Sidney run as well as all stops in the San Juan Islands, the ferry had been fitted out with a similar arrangement as the *Rosario*, including the same lounges, observation rooms and full-service dining room. *[Colorized]*

Before becoming a Port Townsend boat, the *Klickitat* spent decades in the San Juan Islands. For many years, the Steel Electrics were the most versatile vessels in the fleet, able to carry a good load of cars and fit in to nearly any run.

Above left: When the *Evergreen State* arrived in 1954, she deposed the *Kalakala* as the flagship. Every map, schedule and brochure featured stylized renderings of the new ferry, then the largest of its kind in the United States. Originally assigned to the Seattle-Winslow route, the *Evergreen State* moved to the islands full-time in 1959 and for most of her career would call the San Juan Islands home.

Above right: Just who was Ann Green anyway? There to help any traveler, and just a phone call away according to WSF literature, Ann Green didn't exist. Designed as the helpful informational "face" of WSF in the early 1950s, Ann Green faded away without much fanfare by the end of the decade.

A postcard-perfect *Evergreen State* rounds Upright Head on Lopez Island in the early 1960s. For years she was the "big" ferry on the route, not to be surpassed in carrying capacity until 1973.

The *Evergreen State* makes her last arrival in Anacortes on 29 June 2014. It was scheduled to be her *last* trip, but after the farewell trip from the islands, the ferry's retirement lasted a very short time when a major electrical failure on the *Tacoma* and a shortage of vessels resulted in the *Evergreen State* being put back to work. She never did return to the San Juan Islands, but worked for over a year at Vashon Island after she had been "retired." Retired again in 2016, she was sold and was to be moved to the Caribbean. This never happened. As of 2019, she is moored in Olympia under the name *The Dream. [Courtesy of Matt Masuoka]*

The *Vashon*, built in 1930, became the last all-wooden ferry to work for WSF. Spending much of her time in state ownership in the San Juan Islands, she was nicknamed "Old Reliable." One of her more endearing habits was to blow smoke rings from her stack.

The *Vashon*'s passenger cabin in 1971. Perhaps not the most comfortable of cabins, she had originally been built for the short ferry trips between Vashon Island, Fauntleroy, and Harper on the Kitsap Peninsula. Unlike the Steel Electrics, which got padding on the bench seats, the *Vashon*'s all wooden look remained throughout her entire career.

Retired in 1980 and sold in 1982, various plans were proposed for the *Vashon*. She worked as a floating hostel, which wasn't successful, and there was talk of returning her to Friday Harbor on San Juan Island as a floating restaurant. Instead, she was used as a supply vessel in Alaska, where she was wrecked and sunk in 1986.

The only Wood Electric ferry to venture north of Mukilteo, the *Chetzemoka* sailed for a few summers in the San Juan Islands. Seen here in the summer of 1962, the ferry is cruising past James Island. *[Courtesy of BTLS, colorized]*

The *Chippewa* also spent summers in the San Juan Islands and sailing to Sidney, where her limited car deck clearance was less of an issue. Taken in 1957, the photo shows the *Chippewa* backed into the old ferry dock in downtown Anacortes. The Anacortes dock moved to its present location at Ship Harbor in 1960.

No other ferry has had as notorious a history in the San Juan Islands as the *Elwha*. Multiple groundings and dock collisions are among the more colorful incidents in the Super Class ferry's fifty-plus year history. Scheduled to be retired soon, she is one of two vessels certified to sail the international run between Anacortes and Sidney. *[Courtesy of Matt Masuoka]*

The *Yakima* departs from Anacortes in the summer of 2018, sporting her gold fifty-year service stripes. Formerly a Bremerton boat, the *Yakima* has been in the San Juans for over twenty years as of this writing. [*Courtesy of Brandon Moser*]

Opposite above: The Issaquah Class ferry *Chelan* spent her early years in the 1980s opposite the *Yakima* on the Kingston-Edmonds route. Later she began spending time in the San Juan Islands and relieving the other Issaquah Class ferries up and down Puget Sound. In 2005 the ferry was given the necessary upgrades to work the international route between Anacortes and Sidney, relieving the *Evergreen State* from that duty.

Opposite below: Sunrise over Mount Baker bathes the *Chelan* in a warm glow. The Anacortes ferry dock features one of the best views on Puget Sound. [*Courtesy of Brandon Moser*]

The *Samish* is the first newly-built ferry assigned to the San Juan Islands in over two decades. The vessel, which carries the same number of cars as the much older Super Class, has a number of major improvements including wider staircases, two elevators and a far more fuel-efficient propulsion system. *[Courtesy of Brandon Moser]*

144-car ferries are not all equal. Nearly fifty years of design separates these two vessels, the *Samish* on the left and the *Elwha* on the right. Chief among the improvements on the *Samish* are the wide main tunnel, which allows for more trucks and RVs to board the vessel. The *Samish*'s beam is 82 feet; the *Elwha*'s, 73. *[Courtesy of Brandon Moser]*

The *Tillikum*, last of the Evergreen State Class, will finish her career in the San Juan Islands in 2019. She will then be put into reserve status to be used in an emergency before being retired. Currently the oldest ferry in the fleet, she turns sixty in 2019. The ferry is arriving at Friday Harbor in 2018. *[Courtesy of Brandon Moser]*

The little *Guemes* sails from Anacortes to Guemes Island against a stunning sunset. Second vessel of that name and built in 1979, Skagit County is looking to retire the ferry and replace it with an electric-powered vessel.

The *Whatcom Chief* runs between Gooseberry Point on the Lummi Indian Reservation outside Bellingham and Lummi Island. Built in the early 60s, the ferry looks little different today than when this photo was taken in the early 1970s. Whatcom County is looking to replace the *Whatcom Chief* in the next few years.

One of the few long-lasting routes to be discontinued in the north Sound, the Bellingham-Seattle route was served almost exclusively by the passenger steamer *Kulshan*. The opening of better roads made freight cheaper to haul by truck, putting the *Kulshan* and her replacement *Sol Duc* out of work. The run was discontinued in 1935. *[Colorized]*

4

TO CANADA

SEATTLE-VANCOUVER-VICTORIA, SEATTLE-PORT TOWNSEND-PORT ANGELES-VICTORIA, BRITISH COLUMBIA, PORT ANGELES-VICTORIA, SEATTLE-VICTORIA, ANACORTES-SIDNEY, BRITISH COLUMBIA

Ferry routes to Canada from Washington State have long been dominated by steamer. Until the Anacortes-Sidney, British Columbia route was established in 1922, travel to Canada meant either by train or by steamship.

The most elegant of ships to sail the Salish Sea between Seattle and Vancouver and Victoria, British Columbia, were those owned by the Canadian Pacific Railway Company. The "Princess Ships" were nearly all built in the United Kingdom, in some of the same yards that had built such legendary Atlantic floating palaces such as the *Lusitania* and *Mauretania*.

The Puget Sound Navigation Company and Canadian Pacific engaged in a rate war before the First World War that dropped ticket prices to ridiculously low rates, eating into the profits of both companies. After the war, PSN concentrated on its ferry operations but still ran excursions to Vancouver, even though the direct daily route from Seattle to Canada disappeared after WWI.

THE TRIANGLE ROUTE: SEATTLE-VANCOUVER-VICTORIA

Exclusively the domain of the Canadian Pacific, the route running between Seattle, Vancouver, and Victoria, British Columbia had been handled by a number of the larger steamers in the company, most notably the *Princess Charlotte* and *Princess Victoria*. The two were not sister ships, however, and CP planned a new, larger duo to hold down the run. Named *Princess Irene* and *Princess Margaret*, the two would never see service on the Pacific Coast. WWI saw both vessels requisitioned; the *Princess Irene*, a mine-layer, blew up in May 1915. The *Margaret* was scrapped after her war service, Canadian Pacific deciding to build new steamers.

In 1925 the *Princess Marguerite (I)* and *Princess Kathleen* arrived on the Triangle Route, sisters in every way. Handsome vessels with three funnels, they became an immediate success and sailed up until the start of the Second World War. The *Princess Marguerite (I)* would be lost in the war, leaving the *Kathleen* to hold down the Triangle Route on her own, paired with a much older sister ship until the *Princess Patricia* and second *Princess Marguerite* arrived in 1948.

Sadly, the *Princess Kathleen* would meet her end just after WWII, running aground on Lena Point in Alaska and sinking in September 1952.

The *Maggie* and the *Pat* would continue on the Triangle route until it was discontinued in 1958, becoming a summer-only Seattle-Victoria run through 1962. After the end of the summer service in 1962, the *Patricia* would be remodeled for cruising to Alaska.

In the winters of 1965-66, the *Princess Patricia* would be chartered by the newly formed Princess Cruises for excursions from Los Angeles to Acapulco. The cruises proved popular enough that by 1967 a larger vessel was needed; *Princess Patricia* wound up starting a huge operation that continues to this day. She went back to cruises to Alaska and was scrapped in 1995.

The *Princess Marguerite (II)* would continue summer service between Victoria and Seattle under a number of different owners throughout the 1970s and 1980s. Withdrawn for the 1980 season, she was replaced by the repainted British Columbia ferry *Queen of Prince Rupert* which sailed for a single summer season as the *Victoria Princess*. The *Maggie* returned the following year after a major refurbishment.

Paired with the *Princess of Vancouver*, renamed the *Vancouver Island Princess*, for her last two summer seasons, the beloved *Princess Marguerite (II)* would be withdrawn from service for the final time in 1989. She would be scrapped in 1997 at Alang, India.

With the *Princess Marguerite (II)* gone, direct auto service between Seattle and Victoria was tried twice more with B.C. Ferries' *Queen of Burnaby*. First leased by the Royal Victoria Line, the ferry was given a multi-million-dollar refurbishing and sailed as the *Royal Victorian* for the summer of 1994. The company folded after one season, with Clipper Navigation picking up the reins for the following year. As the *Princess Marguerite III*, the ferry ran for three years, netting a two million-dollar loss for Clipper. Auto service from Seattle to Victoria was discontinued after the 1999 season and has not been continued since.

THE NIGHT FERRY: SEATTLE-PORT TOWNSEND-PORT ANGELES-VICTORIA

Running at a slightly slower pace, both Black Ball and Canadian Pacific ran ferries that departed Seattle during the night and arrived in Victoria the following morning, via Port Townsend and Port Angeles. Canadian Pacific started with the *Princess Adelaide* and *Princess Alice*; Black Ball utilized the *Sol Duc*.

Unfortunately, the *Sol Duc* was a heavy roller. In addition, she couldn't hold more than a few cars. With the *Olympic (I)* (ex-*Sioux*) freed up to carry autos on the day run, Black Ball rebuilt the steamer *Iroquois* to become the new night ferry. She took over in 1928.

Canadian Pacific had two handsome steamers replace the *Princess Adelaide* and *Princess Alice* in 1930. From then until the route was discontinued in 1958, the *Princess Elizabeth* and *Princess Joan* would compete on the route.

THE *CHINOOK*

Designed by William Francis Gibbs, who would go on to design the famed S.S. *United States*, the M/V *Chinook* replaced the *Iroquois* in 1947. Described by Gibbs with some hyperbole as "the *Queen Elizabeth* of the Inland Seas," the gleaming white *Chinook* was indeed a special vessel. With room for 100 cars and staterooms for over 200 passengers, the ferry was the epitome of post-war modern. Fitted out by Fredrick and Nelson, Seattle's premier department store, the *Chinook*'s interior was bright and colorful, painted in shades of lacquered green, yellow, and blue. With several lounges, a snack bar, and a full-service, formal dining room, the ferry was a huge hit, solidly booked from the moment it took to the water.

END OF THE NIGHT BOATS

While Canadian Pacific would soldier on, Captain Peabody had all but left Puget Sound in 1951. Only the *Chinook* sailed on, departing Seattle at midnight every night. Gradually, the run was reduced. First Port Townsend was dropped, and finally departures from Seattle. By 1954, the *Chinook* was making several crossings daily between Victoria and Port Angeles. With Captain Peabody's ferry operations in Canada doing a very good turn of business, and the Horseshoe Bay-Nanaimo run needing a second vessel to run with the new *Kahloke*, Peabody announced that the *Chinook*, now shorn of her bow, would be moving to the Nanaimo run.

The city leaders of Port Angeles and Victoria were horrified. They appealed to Washington State Ferries to step in to take over service, at least for the busy summer tourist season. The State agreed, with the understanding that a private operator would take over the service as soon as feasible.

PORT ANGELES-VICTORIA

In the summer of 1955, the *Kalakala* was moved to the crossing between Port Angeles and Victoria. The twenty-year-old streamliner was greeted with great fanfare upon arrival, and for the next five summers, the *Kalakala* would ferry passengers and cars between the two cities. Curiously, the open stretch of water allowed for the engine to run uniformly for a much longer period of time, and the ferry's legendary vibration, which had been curtailed a great deal by the addition of a five-blade propeller, smoothed out even further on the Port Angeles run.

Black Ball Transport, formerly a subsidiary of the Puget Sound Navigation Company, had been operating a fleet of freight trucks and running the old *Iroquois*, turned into a diesel freighter, on the "paper route" hauling paper from the mill at Port Townsend to Victoria for a number of years. No longer suitable to haul cars and passengers, the company built a new vessel specifically for the Port Angeles-Victoria run. The *Coho*, named for the salmon (and perhaps sticking with the fish theme, as "chinook" is also a salmon) arrived on the run in December 1959—and has been sailing the Port Angeles-Victoria run ever since.

ANACORTES-SIDNEY, BRITISH COLUMBIA

Established in 1922, the ferry run between Anacortes and Sidney, British Columbia, started as a summer-only service by Captain Harry Crosby with a converted kelp harvester, proved to be an immediate success. Crosby needed a larger vessel for the next season, so he chartered the *City of Angeles* from Black Ball the following year.

Black Ball purchased the run from Crosby in 1924, operating it seasonally from then on, using some of their plushest auto ferries on the route such as the *Rosario* and *Quilcene*. Traffic continued to build on the run, necessitating larger vessels such as the *Vashon*, which continued the service through World War II.

State ownership saw the largest vessel assigned to the route when the *Evergreen State* became the international ferry in the late 1950s. The route became year-round in 1959.

The *Walla Walla* would make the Sidney run during her one summer in the San Juan Islands, to be replaced by the *Kaleetan* the following year. The *Kaleetan* would be replaced by the *Elwha*, which continues on the run today, the *Chelan* taking over for part of the year.

An easy target during tough economic times, the nearly century-old run has been threatened with discontinuation in nearly every decade from the 1970s onward. However, the financial benefit to Anacortes, the San Juan Islands, and Sidney generated in tourist revenue from the scenic route cannot be disputed, running into the millions of dollars each year.

A compromise was struck in 2003, closing the route for the winter season. The run now operates from late March until early January.

DEFUNCT ROUTE: BELLINGHAM-VICTORIA

For a brief time, Black Ball tried a run between Bellingham and Victoria, using the *Olympic (I)*; the route proved uneconomical and was quickly dropped. The *Olympic (I)* returned to the Port Angeles run, where she continued on her duty as the "day boat" between Port Angeles and Victoria until she was sold in 1941.

The SHADOWING OLYMPICS

Right: The *Princess Victoria* was a dowager by the time this post-WWII menu came out, but for many years she was the most luxurious vessel on the Triangle Route between Seattle, Vancouver, and Victoria, British Columbia.

Below: Though she had been sponsored out to carry about sixty cars, loading the vessel was cumbersome and time consuming. Seen here with the *Motor Princess*, the *Princess Victoria* is laid up and soon to be sold. She would be cut down to a barge and later sink while working in that capacity in 1953.

The slightly larger *Princess Charlotte* ran with the *Princess Victoria* in the years leading up to WWI. After being replaced by the *Princess Kathleen* and *Marguerite (I)* the handsome three-stacker would cruise to Alaska. Sold in 1949 to the Typaldos Bros. Steamship Co. and rebuilt as a single-funnel ship, she sailed under the name *Mediterranean* until being scrapped in 1965. *[Colorized]*

From 1925 until the Second World War, the Triangle Route was the domain of the handsome sisters *Princess Kathleen* and *Princess Marguerite (I)*. Tremendously popular ships, the "pocket liners" would sail successfully all through the Depression. Requisitioned for war service, the *Princess Marguerite (I)* would be lost during the war.

Right: The *Princess Kathleen* would be paired with the *Princess Charlotte* or *Victoria* after WWII until proper replacements could be built. *Princess Patricia* and the second *Princess Marguerite* would relieve the *Kathleen* to do Alaska cruises. Unfortunately, the *Princess Kathleen* would run aground and sink in Alaskan waters in 1952.

Below: The second *Princess Marguerite* was definitely of pre-war design, but that didn't stop her from becoming a beloved vessel. The Triangle Route would eventually be reduced to a direct route from Seattle to Victoria, and the *Marguerite* would solider on alone starting in the early 1960s.

The *Princess Marguerite (II)* meets the *Klickitat* in Admiralty Inlet. Having changed owners several times over the years, she ran with the former *Princess of Vancouver* for a time, and then for Stena Line with the *Vancouver Island Princess*. The final year of service was a financial disaster, prompting the venerable *Marguerite* to be sold. She was scrapped in 1997.

Both the *Princess Marguerite (II)* and *Patricia* looked particularly attractive in their original livery. Virtually identical when built, the *Patricia*, seen here, could be identified by her whistles, which were higher up on the funnels than the *Marguerite (II)*.

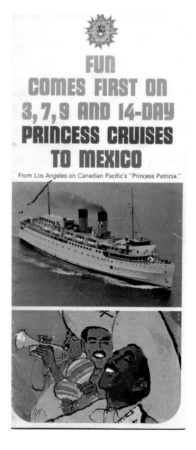

Above: With the end of the Triangle Route, the *Princess Patricia* turned to cruising—first to Alaska and then to Mexico. Here the *Princess Patricia* arrives in San Francisco in 1966.

Right: Few could probably have guessed that when the unpretentious *Princess Patricia* took that first cruise to Mexico that she would be launching the start of one of the biggest cruise lines in the industry. Princess Cruises, which took its name from the *Princess Patricia*, now has a fleet of cruise ships that could fit the *Princess Patricia* neatly inside them, several times over.

FUN COMES FIRST ON 3, 7, 9 AND 14-DAY PRINCESS CRUISES TO MEXICO

From Los Angeles on Canadian Pacific's "Princess Patricia."

The last ship built for Canadian Pacific's British Columbia Service, the *Princess of Vancouver* had been designed to carry autos as well rail cars. That service having ended, and having switched owners several times, she was renamed *Vancouver Island Princess* to run on the Seattle-Victoria route. Losing money on the service, the ferry was retired in 1990.

Stena, which had been operating the *Princess Marguerite* and *Vancouver Island Princess,* brought in the *Crown Princess Victoria* (ex-*Patricia* of the Swedish Lloyd Line) to bolster business. Instead, they ended up shutting down the route entirely and selling the company, ending direct car ferry service between Seattle and Victoria. Photographed in Seattle, the *Skagit* or *Kalama,* then nearly brand new, is in the foreground. *[Courtesy of Shawn J. Dake]*

The *Crown Princess Victoria* was a lovely ship, offering first-class service on its runs to Victoria. Stena decided to cut its losses after losing $10 million on the operation. *[Courtesy of Shawn J. Dake]*

Direct car ferry service from Seattle to Victoria was tried twice more, both utilizing B.C. Ferries' extensively refitted *Queen of Burnaby*. First as the *Royal Victorian* (pictured here, arriving in Seattle) in 1994, which couldn't make any money and shut down in 1997, and then for Clipper Navigation, operating as the *Princess Marguerite III*. After two years, Clipper Navigation gave up, ending car ferry service between the two cities, likely for good. *[Courtesy of Brandon Moser]*

PSN's "Night Boat" service to Victoria began with the 1912-built *Sol Duc*. Departing at midnight, the steamer would stop at Port Townsend and Port Angeles before sailing to Victoria. Despite being a roller in heavy seas, the steamer stayed on the run nearly her entire career.

Iroquois, which had been sold and then purchased back by PSN, was entirely rebuilt in 1928 for the Night Boat run. Rebuilt to carry about 45 cars, the vessel proved to be an immediate success. *[Colorized]*

One of the longest-lived vessels on Puget Sound, the *Iroquois* spent her last years hauling paper and other cargo to Victoria. Having been converted to diesel freighter in the early 50s, she emerged from the rebuilt as one of the most bizarre-looking vessels to ever sail Puget Sound.

"The *Queen Elizabeth* of the Inland Seas" was how William F. Gibbs described the *Chinook*, which he designed for PSN. The first modern vessel to arrive on Puget Sound after WWII, the *Chinook* was a huge hit as soon as she replaced the venerable *Iroquois* and was fully booked for the first several years of service.

Fitted out by Seattle's premier department store, Frederick and Nelson, the *Chinook*'s public rooms were bright, airy, and comfortable. Perhaps garish by today's standards, the ferry was an excellent example of post-war American decor before aesthetics changed in the 1950s.

Staterooms on the *Chinook* were small but comfortable, and equally as colorful. Artwork through the vessel depicted the flora of the Pacific Northwest. The *Chinook* had staterooms for 200 passengers.

Competition on the Night Boat run came from Canadian Pacific, which ran the 1930-built *Princess Joan* and *Princess Elizabeth* on the route. Slower than the *Princess Kathleen* and *Marguerite (I)*, they were designed for a more leisurely pace to Victoria.

Overnight service ended in 1959. The *Princess Joan* was sold to the Epirotiki Line in Greece. Rebuilt as a single-funnel ship and renamed *Hermes*, she sailed until the early 1970s, finally being scrapped in 1974.

Seen here off Port Angeles in the mid-50s, the *Princess Elizabeth* was a sister to the *Joan* in every sense. Two of the loveliest "pocket liners" to sail Puget Sound, they were distinguishable from the *Princess Kathleen* and *Marguerite (I)* by their slightly offset funnels.

Sold at the same time as her sister, the *Princess Elizabeth* became the *Pegasus* for Epirotiki. Both ships were successful in their second life, operating well over a decade for their new owners. The former *Princess Elizabeth* was scrapped in 1976.

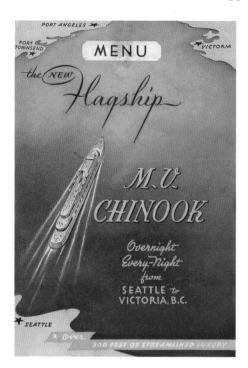

MENU

the NEW *Flagship*

M.V. CHINOOK

*Overnight
Every-Night
from*
SEATTLE *to*
VICTORIA, B.C.

PORT ANGELES
PORT TOWNSEND
VICTORIA
SEATTLE

Over
300 FEET OF STREAMLINED LUXURY

Daily Breakfast Menu
served mornings only

FRUIT JUICE

Fresh Orange	Small 20c	Large 30c
Grapefruit	Small 15c	Large 25c
Tomato	Small 15c	Large 25c

FRUIT

Half Texas Grapefruit	25c
Stewed Prunes	20c

CEREALS

Hot Cereal with Cream	20c
Dry Cereal with Cream	20c

BREAKFAST SPECIALS

Grilled Ham and Eggs, any style, Potatoes and Toast	1.00
Grilled Bacon and Eggs, any style, Potatoes and Toast	90c
Grilled Pork Sausages and Eggs, any style, Potatoes and Toast	95c
Two Fried, Boiled, or Scrambled Eggs, Potatoes and Toast	50c
Two Poached Eggs on Toast	60c
French Toast, Jelly	60c
Milk Toast	35c
Hot Griddle Cakes, Syrup and Butter	35c
Side Order of Grilled Ham, Bacon, or Pork Sausage	50c
Side Order of One Egg (any style)	20c

TOAST, ROLLS, ETC.

Toast, Plain or Buttered	15c
Butterhorn with Butter	20c
Cinnamon Roll with Butter	20c
Doughnuts	15c

BEVERAGES

Coffee, Tea, Milk, Chocolate, Postum	10c

Minimum Charge 40c

Above left: By 1953, which this menu dates from, PSN had dropped the overnight portion of the run and was operating the *Chinook* directly between Port Angeles and Victoria. Captain Peabody's British Columbia ferry service was becoming very profitable, and with the debut of the *Kahloke* on the Horseshoe Bay-Nanaimo run, he was already thinking of a second ferry for the route.

Above right: One dollar could get you grilled ham and eggs, potatoes, and toast on the *Chinook* in 1953.

Right: Direct service between Port Angeles and Victoria wasn't a new development for PSN. Even with the *Iroquois* on the route, service was supplemented during the day by the *Olympic (I)*. Formerly the *Sioux*, she had been rebuilt to carry cars in the early 1920s. She is moored bow-first at the dock in Victoria. *[Colorized]*

Of all the conversions to auto ferries from passenger steamers, the *Olympic (I)*'s was probably the least invasive. The vessel kept her trim lines and, other than a slight blunting of the bow, her steamer looks. *[Colorized]*

The *Malahat* was rebuilt in 1952 with bow doors to cover the *Chinook* when that vessel went in for maintenance and to haul paper from Port Townsend. However, she handled the rough waters of the Strait of Juan de Fuca so poorly and so thoroughly terrorized her passengers that after autumn of 1952 she wasn't used again. This rare photograph shows her in October of 1952 filling in for the *Chinook* for the first—and last—time. *[Colorized]*

The *Chinook* left the Port Angeles run in 1954, never to return. Shorn of her bow, she joined the *Kahloke* on the Nanaimo route. After a long career with Black Ball and B.C. Ferries (where she was renamed *Sechelt Queen*) the ferry was retired in 1982 after working six years for the B.C. Ministry of Highways.

Renamed *Muskegon Clipper* and returned to the United States, the ferry was scheduled to be converted into a floating casino. The *Chinook* was stripped down to the hull in Alabama in 1997 after fifteen years of neglect. The minor gem designed by the famous William F. Gibbs ended her life all but forgotten.

The *Chinook's* sudden withdrawal in 1954 left Port Angeles and Victoria in a panic. Officials from both cities pleaded with the state to restore service at least on a seasonal basis until a replacement could be built. WSF agreed, and the *Kalakala* sailed between the two ports during the summer from 1955-1959.

The old streamliner was spruced up for service to Victoria, receiving a fresh coat of the silver aluminum paint. A side door had to be cut into her port side to allow loading and unloading of vehicles in Victoria.

In December of 1959, Black Ball Transport, a separate company from the Puget Sound Navigation Company, introduced the *Coho*. Designed by Philip Spaulding, the *Coho* has been on the Port Angeles-Victoria run ever since and will celebrate her sixtieth birthday in 2019.

The *Coho* is pictured here in the mid-1980s, with her last competitor for auto traffic, the *Princess Marguerite (II)*. Today passenger-only service to the United States and Victoria is provided by Clipper Navigation, but the *Coho* stands as the lone auto carrier on the route.

Left: Auto ferry service between Anacortes and Sidney, British Columbia, which is about sixteen miles from Victoria, started in 1922 and continues to the present day. Heavily promoted by PSN, this brochure dates from about 1926.

Below: The *City of Angeles* was the first proper auto ferry on the route, arriving in 1923 and replacing a former kelp processing boat that had been converted to carry cars to Sidney. Later the *Rosario, Quilcene, Quillayute, Klickitat, Vashon, Nisqually, Illahee, Evergreen State*, and *Kaleetan* would make the run, to name a few. *[Colorized]*

Right: Another mid-1920s PSN brochure with a distinctive Art Deco feel to it. PSN considered the "International Circuit" to be a combined auto and ferry route utilizing roads and ports between Sidney or Victoria and Bellingham, Anacortes, Seattle, Edmonds, Port Townsend, Port Ludlow, Bremerton and Port Angeles—Black Ball could get you there one way or the other!

Below: Travel to Sidney in the 1940s must have been a slow prospect, given that the *Vashon*, which is waiting to load cars for the return trip, made all of about 10 knots, or about 12 miles an hour.

The wake of the *Chelan* on the evening sailing from Sidney in mid-September 2007. Perhaps the most beautiful ferry route in the system today, the run continues to be popular with the traveling public and has been providing a meaningful economic link for British Columbia and Washington State for almost a century.

APPENDIX

VESSEL STATISTICS FOR FERRIES

Note: Length, Breadth, Draft measurements are in feet, rounded to the nearest foot.

BAINBRIDGE

BUILT: 1928, Lake Washington Shipyard, Houghton, WA.

PREVIOUS/LATER NAMES: a. *Bainbridge*, b. *Jervis Queen*, c. *BCP #30*

OFFICIAL NUMBER: 194368

L/B/D: 195 x 55 x 15 GROSS/NET TONS: 572/389 PASSENGERS/AUTOS: 600 passengers/ 90 cars (1928) 45 cars (1950s)

PROPULSION: 850 horsepower Washington Estep Diesel. SPEED: 10 knots

NAME TRANSLATION: From the Island of the same name. Bainbridge Island was "discovered" by Commander Charles Wilkes when he traversed Agate Pass, and named it for Capt. William Bainbridge, a naval officer who had been hero of the War of 1812.

FINAL DISPOSITION: Rolled over and sank on Fraser River in 1986; scrapped on site.

BALLARD

BUILT/REBUILT: 1900/1931

PREVIOUS/LATER NAMES: a. *City of Everett*, b. *Liberty*, c. *Ballard*. As floating restaurant: Golden Anchors, Four Winds, Surfside 9.

OFFICIAL NUMBER: 127487

L/B/D: 155 x 30 x 9 GROSS/NET TONS: 226/154 PASSENGERS/AUTOS: 250/40

PROPULSION: Washington Estep Diesel, 650 HP

NAME TRANSLATION: From the city of the same name; named for Capt. William Rankin Ballard, who settled the area in 1882.

FINAL DISPOSITION: Retired as a ferryboat in 1944 to become a floating restaurant on Lake Washington. Later moved to Lake Union. After sinking twice at Lake Union, the former floating restaurant was finally broken up in 1973.

CATHLAMET

YEAR BUILT/REBUILT: 1981/93, Marine Power and Equipment, Seattle, WA.
OFFICIAL NUMBER: 636551 CALL SIGN: WYR7641
L/B/D: 328 x 79 x 17 GROSS/NET TONS: 2477/1910 PASSENGERS/AUTOS: 1200/124
PROPULSION: 2 GE FDM-12 Diesels SPEED: 16 knots
NAME TRANSLATION: From the Kathlamet tribe, the Chinook word *calamet* meaning "stone." It was given to the tribe as its members lived along a rocky stretch of the Columbia River. A city also bears its name.
FINAL DISPOSITION: In service, 2019.

CHELAN

BUILT/REBUILT: 1981/2004, Seattle, WA.
OFFICIAL NUMBER: 643291 CALL SIGN: WRA9001
L/B/D: 328 x 79 x 16 GROSS/NET TONS: 2477/1941
PASSENGERS/AUTOS: 1090 international, 1200 domestic/124
PROPULSION: 2 GE 7 FDM-12 Diesels. SPEED: 16 knots
NAME TRANSLATION: From the Chelan language: Tsill-ane, meaning "deep water." The tribe lived along Lake Chelan, which has a maximum depth of 1,486 feet. A city, county and river also bear the name.
FINAL DISPOSITION: In service, 2019. Currently one of two ferries SOLAS (Safety of Life at Sea) equipped to sail the international route from Anacortes to Sidney, British Columbia.

CHETZEMOKA (I)

BUILT: 1927, General Engineering & Drydock Co., Alameda, CA.
PREVIOUS/LATER NAMES: a. *Golden Poppy*, b. *Chetzemoka*
OFFICIAL NUMBER: 226687 CALL SIGN: WH7379
L/B/D: 240 x 60 x 11 GROSS/NET TONS: 779/479 PASSENGERS/AUTOS: 400/50 cars
PROPULSION: 3 Ingersoll-Rand, Diesel Electric (DC) SPEED: 10 knots
NAME TRANSLATION: Named for the S'Klallam chief who lived near Port Townsend.
FINAL DISPOSITION: Sank under tow off the Washington Coast, 31 May 1977.

CHETZEMOKA (II)

BUILT/REBUILT: 2010, Seattle, WA.
OFFICIAL NUMBER: 1228643 CALL SIGN: WDF5502
L/B/D: 274 x 64 x 11 GROSS/NET TONS: 4623/1400 PASSENGERS/AUTOS: 750/64 cars
PROPULSION: Diesel SPEED: 16 knots
NAME TRANSLATION: Namesake of both the S'Klallam chief and the first ferry of the same name.
FINAL DISPOSITION: In service, 2019.

CHIMACUM

BUILT/REBUILT: 2017, Seattle, WA.
OFFICIAL NUMBER: 1266319 CALL SIGN: WDI5854
L/B/D: 362 x 82 x 18 GROSS/NET TONS: 3694/3070 PASSENGERS/AUTOS: 1500/144
PROPULSION: 2 diesel engines SPEED: 17 knots
NAME TRANSLATION: Named after the tribe (now considered extinct and exact meaning unknown).
FINAL DISPOSITION: In service, 2019.

CHINOOK

BUILT: 1947, Todd Shipyard, Seattle WA.
PREVIOUS/LATER NAMES: a. *Chinook*, b. *Chinook II*, c. *Sechelt Queen*, d. *Muskegon Clipper*
OFFICIAL NUMBER: 252908 CALL SIGN: WA3646
L/B/D: 318 x 65 x 17 GROSS/NET TONS: 4106/2792
PASSENGERS/AUTOS: 1000-day passengers, 208 in state rooms/100
PROPULSION: 4 General Electric 278-A engines, diesel electric SPEED: 18.5 knots
NAME TRANSLATION: Name of the jargon from which the ferries derive their names; a warm wind.
FINAL DISPOSITION: Scrapped about 1997.

CHINOOK (II) (passenger-only vessel)

BUILT: 1998, Dakota Creek Industries, Anacortes, WA.
PREVIOUS/LATER NAMES: a. *Chinook*, b. *Golden Gate*
OFFICIAL NUMBER: 1063252 CALL SIGN: WDF7183
L/B/D: 143 x 39 x 5 GROSS/NET TONS: 99/67 PASSENGERS/AUTOS: 450/0
PROPULSION: Diesel waterjet SPEED: 36 knots
NAME TRANSLATION: Named for the first vessel of the same name; a warm wind.
FINAL DISPOSITION: In service at San Francisco as the *Golden Gate*, 2019.

CHIPPEWA

BUILT/REBUILT: 1900/1926/1932, Toledo, OH and Houghton, WA.
OFFICIAL NUMBER: 127440 CALL SIGN: WA3651
L/D/B: 212 x 53 x 16
GROSS/NET TONS: 887/603 PASSENGERS/AUTOS: 950/52 cars
PROPULSION: (1900) twin triple-expansion steam; (1932) Busch-Sulzer diesel, direct drive SPEED: 15 knots (diesel)
NAME TRANSLATION: Another name for Ojibwa, a North American Indian people native to the region around Lake Superior. Ojibwa probably means "puckered," which was likely a reference to the tribes' style of moccasins.
FINAL DISPOSITION: Gutted by fire, June 28, 1968. Hull finally cleared away in the 1980s with the sale of the Collinsville Fishing Resort.

CITY OF ANGELES

BUILT: 1906
PREVIOUS/LATER NAMES: a. *City of Long Beach*, b. *City of Angeles*
OFFICIAL NUMBER: 203193
L/B/D: 125 x 35 x 10 GROSS/NET TONS: 442/347 PASSENGERS/AUTOS: /26 cars
PROPULSION: steam, 450 HP
NAME TRANSLATION: For the city of Port Angeles. The bay was named in 1791, by Juan Francisco de Eliza, who called it *de Nuestra Senora de Los Angeles*. A year later, Capt. George Vancouver shortened the rather long Spanish name to the present form.
FINAL DISPOSITION: Scrapped, 1938.

CITY OF BREMERTON

BUILT/ REBUILT: 1901, Everett, WA. Converted to a ferry in 1921.
PREVIOUS/LATER NAMES: a. *Majestic*, b. *Whatcom*, c. *City of Bremerton*
OFFICIAL NUMBER: 93135

L/B/D: 169 x 48 x 14 GROSS/NET TONS: 510/346 PASSENGERS/AUTOS: 1500/60 cars

PROPULSION: triple expansion engine

NAME TRANSLATION: For the city of Bremerton. Bremerton was named for William Bremer, a German immigrant who platted the town, and later sold the land to the US Navy for the Navy Yard.

FINAL DISPOSITION: Scrapped, 1938.

CITY OF SACRAMENTO

BUILT: 1903, Philadelphia, PA/1952 Yarrows, Victoria, British Columbia.

PREVIOUS/LATER NAMES: a. *Asbury Park*, b. *City of Sacramento*, c. *Kahloke*, d. *Langdale Queen*, e. *Lady Grace*

OFFICIAL NUMBER: 107848

L/B/D: 307 x 50 x 15 GROSS/NET TONS: 3016/1829 PASSENGERS/AUTOS: 2000 (as *Kahloke*, 1000)/ 100

NAME TRANSLATIONS: For the California state capitol city. Spanish explorer Gabriel Moraga discovered and named the Sacramento Valley and the Sacramento River in either 1799 or 1808—accounts vary. Moraga wrote, "Canopies of oaks and cottonwoods, many festooned with grapevines, overhung both sides of the blue current. Birds chattered in the trees and big fish darted through the pellucid depths. The air was like champagne, and (the Spaniards) drank deep of it, drank in the beauty around them. "*Es como el sagrado sacramento*!" (It's like the Holy Sacrament.)

FINAL DISPOSITION: Hull sank in 2008; raised and scrapped later that year.

CITY OF TACOMA

BUILT: 1921, Gig Harbor, WA.

OFFICIAL NUMBER: 221831

L/B/D 150 x 44 x 10 GROSS/NET TONS: 269/179 PASSENGERS/AUTOS: 300/50 cars

HISTORY: Auto ferry service began on the Narrows route between Tacoma and Gig Harbor in 1921 when the Skansie Brothers completed the *City of Tacoma*. Re-engined as a diesel in 1927. Retired and sold, 1951. Served as a floating breakwater and storage barge at Lake Washington Marina.

NAME TRANSLATION: For the city of Tacoma (see *Tacoma*).

FINAL DISPOSITION: Sank at Yarrow Bay, July 1969. The old ferry is a popular dive site.

COHO

BUILT: 1959, Seattle WA.

OFFICIAL NUMBER: 280243 CALL SIGN: WM4599

L/B/D: 342 x 72 x 13 GROSS/NET TONS: 5366/3897 PASSENGERS/AUTOS: 1000/110 cars

NAME TRANSLATION: Named for the salmon, which are also known as silver salmon.

FINAL DISPOSITION: In service, Port Angeles to Victoria, British Columbia as of 2019.

CROSLINE

BUILT/REBUILT: 1925/1947 (conversion to double-ender), Marine Construction Company, Seattle, WA.

OFFICIAL NUMBER: 224839 CALL SIGN: WH7219

L/B/D: 151 x 55 x 11 GROSS/NET TONS: 466/316 PASSENGERS/AUTOS: 300/30 cars

PROPULSION: Diesel SPEED: 10 knots

NAME TRANSLATION: Taken from Captain Crosby's name, the "C" in the A-B-C scheme.

FINAL DISPOSITION: Broken up about 1977.

CROWN PRINCESS VICTORIA

BUILT/REBUILT: 1966/78 Ab Lindholmen Varv, Gothenburg, Sweden, Smiths Dock Company, Tyneside, England.

PREVIOUS/LATER NAMES: a. *Patricia*, b. *Stena Oceanica*, c. *Stena Saga*, d. *Lion Queen*, e. *Crown Princess Victoria*, f. *Pacific Star*, g. *Sun Fiesta*, h. *Lion Queen*, i. *Amusement World*

OFFICIAL NUMBER: 6620773 **CALL SIGN:** HOGV

L/B/D: 453 x 74 x 19 **GROSS/NET TONS:** 12764/3924 **PASSENGERS/AUTOS:** 1100 (with crew)/0

PROPULSION: Diesel **SPEED:** 15 knots

NAME TRANSLATION: For the city of Victoria.

FINAL DISPOSITION: In service for New Century Tours, Singapore as a cruise/gambling ship.

DEFIANCE

BUILT: 1927 by the Skansie Brothers Shipyard in Gig Harbor, WA.

OFFICIAL NUMBER: 226366 **CALL SIGN:** WE8648

L/B/D: 165 x 50 x 13 **GROSS/NET TONS:** 444/295 **PASSENGERS/AUTOS:** 300/32 cars

PROPULSION: 2 Fairbanks Morse diesel engines

NAME TRANSLATION: Named for Point Defiance which was named by Cmdr. Charles Wilkes, who stated "This narrow pass was intended by nature for the defense of Puget Sound."

FINAL DISPOSITION: Converted to a dogfish processor, the ferry was listed as being "out of service" in 2006 in Juneau, Alaska; likely scrapped at that time.

ELWHA (I)

BUILT: 1927 by General Engineering & Drydock Co., Alameda, CA.

PREVIOUS/LATER NAMES: a. *Golden Shore*, b. *Elwha*, c. *Silver Strand*

OFFICIAL NUMBER: 226767 **CALL SIGN:** WK4146

L/B/D: 227 x 44 x 16 **GROSS/NET TONS:** 779/479 **PASSENGERS/AUTOS:** 500/55 cars

NAME TRANSLATION: Elk.

FINAL DISPOSITION: Wrecked on Los Angeles breakwater, 30 November 1970.

ELWHA (II)

BUILT/REBUILT: 1968/1991, National Steel and Shipbuilding Co., San Diego, CA/Fisherman's Boat Shop, Everett, WA.

OFFICIAL NUMBER: 512324 **CALL SIGN:** WY3960

L/B/D: 382 x 73 x 19 **GROSS/NET TONS:** 2813/1322

PASSENGERS/AUTOS: 1090 (International), 2000 Domestic/144 cars

PROPULSION: 4 EMD 16-645 BC diesels **SPEED:** 17 knots

NAME TRANSLATION: Elk, and for the first *Elwha*.

FINAL DISPOSITION: In service, 2019.

ENETAI

BUILT: 1927, General Engineering & Drydock Co., Alameda, CA.

FORMER/LATER NAMES: a. *Santa Rosa*, b. *Enetai*, c. *Santa Rosa*

OFFICIAL NUMBER: 226599 **CALL SIGN:** WA4715

L/B/D: 256 x 66 x 13 **GROSS/NET TONS:** 1023/695 **PASSENGERS/AUTOS:** 1500/90 autos

PROPULSION: Busch-Sulzer diesel, 2800 HP (direct drive) **SPEED:** 15 knots

NAME TRANSLATION: "Across, on the other side."

FINAL DISPOSITION: Direct sister to the *Nisqually* and *Quinault*. Returned to San Francisco in 1968 under her original name, *Santa Rosa*. Currently headquarters of Hornblower Yachts and a successful banquet/wedding/reception hall. The *Santa Rosa* is the sole survivor of the Steel Electric class ferries.

EVERGREEN STATE

BUILT/REBUILT: 1954/1988 Puget Sound Bridge & Drydock Co, Todd Shipyard, Seattle, WA.
FORMER/LATER NAMES: a. *Evergreen State*, b. *The Dream*
OFFICIAL NUMBER: D268732 CALL SIGN: WTQ6960
L/B/D: 310 x 73 x 16 GROSS/NET TONS: 2041/1388 PASSENGERS/AUTOS: 875/87 cars
NAME TRANSLATION: State nickname.
FINAL DISPOSITION: Retired in 2014, the ferry was almost immediately put back into service. After an additional year, she was officially retired in December 2015. Sold in March 2017, she was to be moved to the island of Grenada in the Caribbean. This never happened. She moved from Tacoma to the Port of Olympia and was renamed *The Dream*. Plans were to move her to Florida as a floating entertainment venue. She was to be towed to Florida in the summer of 2018. As of this writing, she is still moored at the Port of Olympia.

FOX ISLAND

BUILT: 1925, Skansie Brothers, Gig Harbor, WA.
FORMER/LATER NAMES: a. *Wollochet*, b. *Fox Island*, c. *George S. Pearson*, d. *Western Service*
OFFICIAL NUMBER: 224559
L/B/D: 90 x 33 x 10 GROSS/NET TONS: 148/98 PASSENGERS/AUTOS: 134/18 cars
NAME TRANSLATION: Named for Fox Island, which was named in 1841, by Commander Charles Wilkes for Dr. J. L. Fox, the assistant surgeon of the Wilkes Expedition.
FINAL DISPOSITION: Sold to Canadian interests after the *Defiance* replaced the vessel on the Port Townsend-Keystone run. She sailed as the *George S. Pearson* until retired and sold in 1966. As the *Western Service*, upper works wrecked in a storm in 1968, scrapped thereafter.

GUEMES(II)

BUILT: 1979, Gladding Hearn Shipyard, Somerset, Massachusetts.
OFFICIAL NUMBER: 601686 CALL SIGN: WYW9807
L/B/D: 124 x 34 x 7 GROSS/NET TONS: 91/91
NAME TRANSLATION: Honoring the first *Guemes* and for the Island. See above.
FINAL DISPOSITION: In service, 2019, scheduled to be replaced in the next two to three years.

HIYU (II)

BUILT: 1967, Portland, OR.
OFFICIAL NUMBER: 508159 CALL SIGN: WX9133
L/B/D: 162 x 63 x 11 GROSS/NET TONS: 498/378 PASSENGERS/AUTOS: 200/34 cars
PROPULSION: Caterpillar Diesel, 860 HP SPEED: 10 knots
NAME TRANSLATION: Native American/Chinook: "plenty."
FINAL DISPOSITION: Sold in 2016, currently a floating entertainment venue on Lake Union. (2019)

HYAK

BUILT: 1967, National Steel & Shipbuilding Company, San Diego, CA.
OFFICIAL NUMBER: 508160 CALL SIGN: WX9439
L/B/D: 382 x 73 x 19 GROSS/NET TONS: 2704/1214 PASSENGERS/AUTOS: 2000/144 cars

PROPULSION: Diesel Electric, 8000 HP SPEED: 17 knots
NAME TRANSLATION: Chinook jargon: "fast" or "speedy."
FINAL DISPOSITION: In service, 2019; slated for retirement, 2020.

ILLAHEE

BUILT/REBUILT: 1927/1958/1986, Moore Drydock Co., Oakland, CA/Commercial Ship Repair, Winslow, WA/
Seattle, WA.
PREVIOUS/LATER NAMES: a. *Lake Tahoe*, b. *Illahee*
OFFICIAL NUMBER: 226588 CALL SIGN: WXT9366
L/B/D: 256 x 74 x 13 GROSS/NET TONS:1364/931 PASSENGERS/AUTOS: 616/59 cars (2007 figures)
PROPULSION: Diesel Electric HP: 2896   SPEED: 12 knots
NAME TRANSLATION: Chinook for "land, place, location; ground, earth, dirt."
FINAL DISPOSITION: Scrapped in Ensenada, MX, 2011.

INDIANAPOLIS

BUILT/REBUILT: 1904/1932, Craig Shipyards, Toledo, OH/Lake Washington Shipyard, Houghton, WA.
OFFICIAL NUMBER: 200920 SIGNAL LETTERS: KJNE
L/B/D: 180 x 32 x 19 GROSS/NET TONS: 765/520
PROPULSION: triple-expansion steam engine, 1500 HP SPEED: 16 knots
NAME TRANSLATION: Invented by Indiana Supreme Court Justice Jeremiah Sullivan, who joined Indiana with
polis, the Greek word for city; Indianapolis literally means "Indiana City."
FINAL DISPOSITION: Scrapped 1938.

IROQUOIS

BUILT/REBUILT: 1901/1928, Craig Shipyards, Toledo, OH/Lake Washington Shipyard, Houghton, WA.
OFFICIAL NUMBER: 100730 SIGNAL LETTERS: KVSB/KJNK (1933)
L/B/D: 214 x 34 x 15 (as built; 214 x 49 x 15 in 1928) PASSENGERS/AUTOS: 400 day passengers, 160 night
passengers in 53 cabins/40-50 cars
NAME TRANSLATION: From the Iroquois tribe, also known as the *Haudenosaunee*, and to themselves, the
Goano'ganoch'sa'jeh'seroni or *Ganonsyon*. A historically powerful important Native American people who
formed the Iroquois Confederacy, a league of five (six after 1722) the Five Nations and Five Nations of the
Iroquois distinct nations. The name means "Heart people, people of God."
FINAL DISPOSITION: Scuttled, 1982.

ISLANDER

BUILT: 1924, Wilson Shipbuilding Company, Astoria, OR.
PREVIOUS/LATER NAMES: a. *Tourist No. 2*, b. *Octopus*, c. *Tourist No. 2*, d. *Islander*, e. *Kirkland*, f. *Tourist No. 2*
OFFICIAL NUMBER: 223916 CALL SIGN: WB3893
L/B/D: 110 x 36 x 8 GROSS/NET TONS: 95/65 PASSENGERS/AUTOS:155/20
PROPULSION: 320 HP Atlas-Imperial diesel engine
NAME TRANSLATION: Named for use on the Pierce County ferry system, serving Anderson and Ketron Islands.
FINAL DISPOSITION: Built as the *Tourist No. 2* for the Astoria-Megler route. To Pierce County, 1967-1996.
Purchased by Argosy Cruises, renamed *Kirkland*. Damaged by fire, 2010; sold. Repaired to working condition,
returned to Astoria, 2016, restoration underway.

ISSAQUAH (II)

BUILT/REBUILT: 1979/1989, Marine Power & Equipment, Seattle, WA.
OFFICIAL NUMBER: 624022   CALL SIGN: WSD3625
L/B/D: 328 x 79 x 17 GROSS/NET TONS: 2469/1739 PASSENGERS/AUTOS: 1200/124
PROPULSION: 2 GE 7 FDM-12 diesels, variable pitch propellers SPEED: 16 knots
NAME TRANSLATION: From the Samish/Snoqualmie Tribes, Lushoot dialect: "place of the Squak People."
FINAL DISPOSITION: In service, 2019.

KALAKALA

BUILT/REBUILT: 1926/1935 Moore Drydock Co, Oakland, CA/Lake Washington Shipyard, Houghton, WA.
PREVIOUS/LATER NAMES: a. *Peralta*, b. *Kalakala*
OFFICIAL NUMBER: 226244 CALL SIGN: WA6703
L/B/D: 277 x 56 x 16 GROSS/NET TONS: 1417/963 PASSENGERS/AUTOS: 1943/110 cars (as built 1935, about 65 in 1967)
PROPULSION: direct drive Busch-Sulzer diesel, 3000 HP SPEED: 16 knots
NAME TRANSLATION: Chinook jargon, "Flying Bird."
FINAL DISPOSITION: Scrapped 2015.

KALAMA

BUILT: 1989, Halter Marine, New Orleans, LA
OFFICIAL NUMBER: D949139   CALL SIGN: WAA6310
L/B/D: 112 x 25 x 8 GROSS/NET TONS: 96/65 PASSENGERS/AUTOS: 230/0
NAME TRANSLATION: From the Calama language: "pretty maiden."
FINAL DISPOSITION: After the *Skagit* sinking, the *Kalama* was sold to operators unknown. Her status is listed as "active." As of January 2018, she was at the island of Anjouan, an autonomous high island in the Indian Ocean.

KALEETAN

BUILT/REBUILT: 1967/1999 National Steel and Shipbuilding Company, San Diego, CA. Lake Union Drydock/Todd Shipyard, Seattle, WA
OFFICIAL NUMBER: D508604. CALL SIGN: WY2512
L/B/D: 382 x 73 x 19 GROSS/NET TONS: 2704/1214 PASSENGERS/AUTOS: 2000/144
PROPULSION: 4 EMD 645 Diesel Electric, 8000 HP SPEED: 17 knots
NAME TRANSLATION: Chinook, "arrow."
FINAL DISPOSITION: In service, 2019.

KEHLOKEN

BUILT: 1926, General Engineering & Drydock Co., Alameda, CA
PREVIOUS/LATER NAMES: a. *Golden State*, b. *Kehloken*
OFFICIAL NUMBER: 225772 CALL SIGN: WH6755
L/B/D: 240 x 60 x 13 GROSS/NET TONS: 780/481 PASSENGERS/AUTOS: 770/50
PROPULSION: Ingersoll Rand Diesel electric, 1200 HP SPEED: 10 knots
NAME TRANSLATION: Swan.
FINAL DISPOSITION: Gutted by fire, September 19, 1979. Later cleaned up and towed out to Possession Point and sunk as an artificial reef.

KENNEWICK

BUILT: 2011, Seattle, WA.
OFFICIAL NUMBER: 1229902 CALL SIGN: WDF6991
L/B/D: 274 x 64 x 11 GROSS/NET TONS: 4623/1887 PASSENGERS/AUTOS: 750/64
PROPULSION: Diesel SPEED: 16 knots
NAME TRANSLATION: Native American for "winter paradise, winter haven; grassy place, grassy slope."
FINAL DISPOSITION: In service, 2019.

KITSAP (I)

BUILT: 1925 Lake Washington Shipyard, Houghton, WA
OFFICIAL NUMBER: 224849 CALL SIGN: WA6847
L/B/D: 166 x 51 x 9 GROSS/NET TONS: 525/258 PASSENGERS/AUTOS: 325/95 cars in 1920s, 44 by 1960
PROPULSION: Washington Estep Diesel, 600 HP. SPEED: 9 knots
NAME TRANSLATION: Named for chief Kitsap, meaning "brave."
FINAL DISPOSITION: Sank under tow in Alaska, 1966.

KITSAP (II)

BUILT/ REBUILT: 1980/1992, Marine Power & Equipment/Lake Union Dry Dock, Seattle, WA
OFFICIAL NUMBER: 630023 CALL SIGN: WYR3421
L/B/D: 328 x 79 x 17 GROSS/NET TONS: 2475/1755 PASSENGERS/AUTOS: 1200/124
PROPULSION: 2 GE 7 FDM-12 diesels, variable pitch propellers, 5000 HP   SPEED: 16 knots
NAME TRANSLATION: Named for Chief Kitsap and the first ferry with that name.
FINAL DISPOSITION: In service, 2019.

KITTITAS

BUILT/REBUILT: 1980/1990 Marine Power & Equipment Seattle WA/
OFFICIAL NUMBER: D627507 CALL SIGN: WYQ9302
L/B/D: 328 x 79 x 17 GROSS/NET TONS: 2476/1756 PASSENGERS/AUTOS: 1200/124 cars
PROPULSION: 2 GE 7 FDM-12 diesels, variable pitch propellers, 5000 HP SPEED: 16 knots
NAME TRANSLATION: name is from the Native American word K'tatus, meaning "gray gravel bank"; it refers to an extensive gravel bank on a river shoal near Ellensburg.
FINAL DISPOSITION: In service, 2019.

KLAHANIE

BUILT: 1928, General Engineering & Drydock Co., Alameda, CA
PREVIOUS/LATER NAMES: a. *Golden Age*, b. *Klahanie*
OFFICIAL NUMBER: 227249 CALL SIGN: WG7101
L/B/D: 241 x 57 x 11' GROSS/NET TONNAGE: 779/480 PASSENGERS/AUTOS: 601/55
PROPULSION: Ingersoll Rand, Diesel Electric, 1200 HP SPEED: 10 knots
NAME TRANSLATION: Chinook, "great out of doors."
FINAL DISPOSITION: Upper works destroyed by fire, July 29, 1990; hull broken up by the Department of Natural Resources as part of the Duwamish River habitat restoration, 1998.

KLAHOWYA

BUILT/REBUILT: 1958/1995 Puget Sound Bridge and Drydock Co, Seattle, WA.
OFFICIAL NUMBER: D277872 CALL SIGN: WK7107
L/B/D: 310 x 73 x 16 GROSS/NET TONS: 2055/1397 PASSENGERS/AUTOS: 800/ 100 cars as built, 87 by 2018
PROPULSION: Diesel Electric, 2500 HP SPEED: 13 knots
NAME TRANSLATION: Chinook, "greetings", or "how do you do?"
FINAL DISPOSITION: Retired in 2017. Awaiting disposal as of 2018.

KLICKITAT

BUILT/REBUILT: 1927/1958/1981 Bethlehem Shipbuilding Union Yard, San Francisco, CA/ Commercial Ship Repair, Winslow, WA/Tacoma, WA.
PREVIOUS/LATER NAMES: a. *Stockton*, b. *Klickitat*
OFFICIAL NUMBER: 226567 CALL SIGN: WA6855
L/B/D: 256 x 74 x 13 GROSS/NET TONS: 1408/957 PASSENGERS/AUTOS: 616/64 (2007)
PROPULSION: Diesel-Electric SPEED: 12 knots
NAME TRANSLATION: "Beyond." Also, one of the Native American names for Mount Adams.
FINAL DISPOSITION: Scrapped in Ensenada MX, 2009.

KULSHAN (I)

BUILT: 1910 Moran Shipbuilders, Seattle, WA
OFFICIAL NUMBER: 207780 SIGNAL LETTERS: LBPT/KJPG by 1932
L/B/D: 160 x 32 x 20 GROSS/NET TONS: 926/563
PROPULSION: One triple expansion steam engine, developing 1100 HP SPEED: 16 knots
NAME TRANSLATION: Native American name for Mount Baker; various meanings, including, "white sentinel" and "shot at the point."
FINAL DISPOSITION: Scrapped, 1938.

KULSHAN (II)

BUILT: 1954 Oakland, CA.
PREVIOUS/LATER NAMES: a. *Crown City*, b. *Kulshan*, c. *Governor*
OFFICIAL NUMBER: 267527 CALL SIGN: WF6787
L/B/D: 242 x12 x 65 GROSS/NET TONS: 678/352 PASSENGERS/AUTOS: 350/65
NAME TRANSLATION: For the steamer of the same name; Native American name for Mount Baker; various meanings, including, "white sentinel" and "shot at the point."
FINAL DISPOSITION: As of 2019, in service as the *Governor* at for the Martha's Vineyard Steamship Authority.

LESCHI

BUILT: 1913, J. F. Duthie & Company, Seattle, WA.
OFFICIAL NUMBER: 211875 CALL SIGN: WH6752
L/B/D: 170 x 50 x 9 GROSS/NET TONS: 336/228 PASSENGERS:/AUTOS: 453/40
PROPULSION: Originally steam paddle wheel. Rebuilt as diesel, 560HP.   SPEED: 10 knots
NAME TRANSLATION: named for the chief of the Nisqually tribe.
FINAL DISPOSITION: Blown ashore in a storm, 1978; abandoned. Hulk still is on the beach and visible in Shotgun Cove, Alaska as of 2014.

LINCOLN

BUILT: 1914, Lake Washington Shipyard, Houghton Washington, for King County on Lake Washington.

OFFICIAL NUMBER: 212845

L/B/D: 147x 43 x 13, GROSS/NET TONS: 580/394 PASSENGERS/AUTOS: ?/32 cars

PROPULSION: Steam powered, 800 hp.

NAME TRANSLATION: Named for President Lincoln.

FINAL DISPOSITION: Converted into a barge in 1955 by the Pacific Pearl Company of Alaska. Out of documentation as of 1957, and likely scrapped at that time.

MALAHAT

BUILT: 1910, San Francisco, CA.

PREVIOUS/LATER NAMES: a. *Napa Valley*, b. *Malahat*

OFFICIAL NUMBER: 207420 SIGNAL LETTERS: KERW

L/B/D: 231 x 49 x 15 GROSS/NET TONS: 991/673 PASSENGERS/AUTOS: 1528/75

PROPULSION: Triple expansion Steam engine, 2600 HP

NAME TRANSLATION: Name of a Coast Salish group on southern Vancouver Island, British Columbia, Canada.

FINAL DISPOSITION: Destroyed by fire, Portland, Oregon, 1956.

MOTOR PRINCESS

BUILT: 1923, Yarrows, British Columbia, Canada.

PREVIOUS/LATER NAMES: a. *Motor Princess*, b. *Pender Queen*, c. *Pender Lady*

OFFICIAL NUMBER: 180894

L/B/D: 153 x 44 x 9 GROSS/NET TONS: 428/291 (final) PASSENGERS/AUTOS: 250/40

PROPULSION: one White Superior diesel engine, 1050 HP SPEED: 9 knots

NAME TRANSLATION: Named because of its role as an automobile ferry and because of its diesel propulsion. Later became the ferry *Pender Queen*.

FINAL DISPOSITION: 1955: Sold to Gulf Island Ferry Company, rebuilt with steel passenger cabin and open car deck. 1961: Sold to B.C. Ferries and renamed *Pender Queen*. Retired in 1980; used as a fish camp; sank in Naden Harbour, Graham Island, British Columbia, 24 June 2003. Raised and broken up, August 2003.

NISQUALLY

BUILT/REBUILT: 1927/1958/1987 Bethlehem Shipbuilding Union Yard, San Francisco, CA/ Commercial Ship Repair, Winslow, WA/Seattle, WA.

PREVIOUS/LATER NAMES: a. *Mendocino*, b. *Nisqually*

OFFICIAL NUMBER: 226712 CALL SIGN: WA8696

L/B/D: 256 x 74 x 13 GROSS/NET TONS: 1490/1013 PASSENGERS/AUTOS: 616/ 59 cars (2007)

PROPULSION: Diesel electric, 2896 HP. SPEED: 12 knots

NAME TRANSLATION: From the tribe, the name of which appears to have been an adaptation of the French-Canadian workers from the Hudson's Bay Company who called the Indians *Nez quarre* which translates to "Square nose." A river, a lake and glacier on Mount Rainier are all named Nisqually.

FINAL DISPOSITION: Scrapped in Ensenada, MX, 2011.

OLYMPIC (I)

BUILT: 1910, Seattle, WA.

PREVIOUS/LATER NAMES: a. *Sioux*, b. *Olympic*, c. *USAT Franklin S. Leisenring*

OFFICIAL NUMBER: 208278 SIGNAL LETTERS: KMVZ

L/B/D: 175 x 39 x 23 GROSS/NET TONS: 1317/896 PASSENGERS/AUTOS: 560/40

PROPULSION: One four-cylinder triple-expansion engine, 1400 HP

NAME TRANSLATION: For the Mountain range; mountains took the name from the tallest peak, Mount Olympus; the name was given by Capt. John Meares who said at the time, "For truly it must be the home of the Gods."

FINAL DISPOSITION: Sold to the US Army, 1941. Renamed *USAT Franklin S Leisenring*. During World War II USAT *Franklin S. Leisenring* was assigned to the Panama Canal Zone. Following World War II *USAT Franklin S. Leisenring* was sold to a Dutch Guiana company for service out of Paramaribo on the Suriname River. According to author Gordon Newell in *Pacific Steamboats* (1958), the *Olympic* ex-*Sioux* was still in service, steaming up and down the Suriname River.

OLYMPIC (II)

BUILT: 1938, Baltimore, MD.

PREVIOUS/LATER NAMES: a. *Governor Harry W. Nice* b. *Olympic*

OFFICIAL NUMBER: 237285 CALL SIGN: WB6081

L/D/W: 208 x 62 x 9 GROSS/NET TONS: 773/308 PASSENGERS/AUTOS: 605/55

PROPULSION: 1 Fairbanks Morse Diesel engine, 1400 HP SPEED: 11 knots

NAME TRANSLATION: For the Mountain range; mountains took the name from the tallest peak, Mount Olympus; the name was given by Capt. John Meares who said at the time, "For truly it must be the home of the Gods."

FINAL DISPOSITION: As of 2019, moored at Anderson Island, WA. Status beyond that unknown.

POTLATCH

BUILT: 1912, Seattle Construction and Drydock Company, Seattle, WA.

OFFICIAL NUMBER: 210378 SIGNAL LETTERS: LCNJ

L/B/D: 150 x 27 x 17 GROSS/NET TONS: 575/325 PASSENGERS/AUTOS:

PROPULSION: Triple Expansion Steam Engine, 600 HP

NAME TRANSLATION: Chinook, to give, or gift.

FINAL DISPOSITION: Scrapped, 1937.

PRINCESS CHARLOTTE

BUILT: 1908, Fairfield Co. Ltd., Glasgow, Scotland.

PREVIOUS/LATER NAMES: a. *Princess Charlotte*, b. *Mediterranean*

L/B/D: 330 x 47 x 24 GROSS/NET TONS: 3926/

NAME TRANSLATION: Named for a granddaughter of Queen Victoria and the daughter of Emperor Frederick of Germany.

FINAL DISPOSITION: Sold to Typaldos Bros. Steamship Co. of Piraeus, Greece, 1949. Renamed *Mediterranean* for service between Turkey, Greece, and Italy and rebuilt with one stack. Scrapped in 1965.

PRINCESS ELIZABETH

BUILT: 1930, Fairfield Co., Glasgow, Scotland.

PREVIOUS/LATER NAMES: a. *Princess Elizabeth*, b. *Pegasus*, c. *Highland Queen*

L/B/D: 365 x 52 x 25 GROSS/NET TONS: 5251/

NAME TRANSLATION: For Princess Elizabeth, now Queen Elizabeth II, elder daughter of King George VI and Queen Elizabeth and the current (2019) Queen of England.

FINAL DISPOSITION: 1961: sold to Epirotiki Line, renamed *Pegasus* and rebuilt with one funnel. 1973: Renamed *Highland Queen*. 1976: Scrapped.

PRINCESS JOAN

BUILT: 1930, Fairfield Co., Glasgow, Scotland.
PREVIOUS/LATER NAMES: a. *Princess Joan*, b. *Hermes*
L/B/D: 365 x 52 x 25 GROSS/NET TONS: 5251/
NAME TRANSLATION: Named for the old steamer *Joan*, which was named for Joan Dunsmuir, wife of Robert Dunsmuir, coal baron and principal in the Esquimalt & Nanaimo Railway on Vancouver Island.
FINAL DISPOSITION: 1961: Sold to Epirotiki Line, renamed *Hermes* and rebuilt with one funnel. 1974: Scrapped.

PRINCESS KATHLEEN

BUILT: 1925, John Brown & Co. Ltd., Clydebank, Scotland
L/B/D: 350 x 60 x 17 GROSS/NET TONS: 5875/
NAME TRANSLATION: Named by Canadian Pacific President Sir Edward Beatty for his life-long friend Miss Kathleen Madill. One of Thomas Shaughnessy's daughters was Marguerite Kathleen Shaughnessy and her name also may well have influenced the choice of the name for the steamer.
FINAL DISPOSITION: Ran aground 7 September 1952 off Lena Point, Alaska and sank. The remaining fuel on the *Princess Kathleen*, some 110,000 gallons of bunker C oil, were removed in May 2010, at the cost of 12 million dollars.

PRINCESS MARGUERITE (I)

BUILT: 1925, John Brown & Co. Ltd., Clydebank, Scotland
L/B/D: 350 x 60 x 17 GROSS/NET TONS: 5875/
NAME TRANSLATION: Named for the Honorable Marguerite Shaughnessy, daughter of the former CPR president, Lord Shaughnessy (formerly Sir Thomas Shaughnessy).
FINAL DISPOSITION: The 5875-ton, 22-knot express steamer *Princess Marguerite*, formerly in operation with the *Princess Kathleen* in the Canadian Pacific B. C. Coast Service on the Seattle- Victoria-Vancouver triangle run, was torpedoed and sunk on 17 August 1942 in the Mediterranean while in operation as a British troopship.

PRINCESS MARGUERITE (II)

BUILT: 1949, Fairfield Co., Glasgow, Scotland.
L/B/D: 373 x 56 x 16 GROSS/NET TONS: 5911/
NAME TRANSLATION: Named to commemorate the first *Princess Marguerite* sunk during WWII.
FINAL DISPOSITION: 1979: Officially retired. 1981: Refurbished, returned to service. 1988: Operations turned over to B.C. Stena Line. 1989: Withdrawn from service for final time after disastrous year under Stena Line. 1992: Converted to gambling ship in Singapore. 1997: scrapped at Alang, India after many failed ventures to return her to service.

PRINCESS PATRICIA (II)

BUILT: 1949, Fairfield Co. Ltd., Glasgow, Scotland.
L/B/D: 356 x 56 x 16 GROSS/NET TONS: 5611 (6062 as cruise ship)/
NAME TRANSLATION: Named to commemorate the first *Princess Patricia*.
FINAL DISPOSITION: 1978: retired from cruise service; 1986: Hotel ship for World's Fair in Vancouver, B.C. 1995: Scrapped.

PRINCESS OF VANCOUVER

BUILT: 1955, A. Stephen & Sons, Ltd., Glasgow, Scotland.
PREVIOUS/LATER NAMES: a. *Princess of Vancouver*, b. *Vancouver Island Princess*, c. *Princess of Vancouver*, d. *Nan Hai Ming Zhu* e. *Pearl of the South China Sea*
OFFICIAL NUMBER: 5284998
L/B/D: 416 x 66 x15 GROSS/NET TONS: 5554/
NAME TRANSLATION: Named in complementary fashion for the other major city on the Vancouver-to-Nanaimo service for which the vessel was built.
FINAL DISPOSITION: 1981: Sold to Ministry of Highways. 1985: to B.C. Ferries. 1987: Sold to B.C. Steamship Company and renamed *Vancouver Island Princess*. 1989: Sold to Stena Line. 1990: Retired. 1993: Sold to Stephanie Shipping, China, renamed *Nan Hai Ming Zhu*. 2001: Sold to Haveton Shipping of Hong Kong, renamed *Pearl of the South China Sea*. 2007: Listed as being in active service.

PRINCESS VICTORIA

BUILT: 1903, Swan & Hunter Ltd, Newcastle, England.
L/B/D: 300 x 58 x 15 GROSS/NET TONS: 3167/
NAME TRANSLATION: Named for Princess Victoria, daughter of King Edward VII and the granddaughter of Queen Victoria. The recent death of Queen Victoria and the fact that Victoria was the headquarters of the new steamship service also made the name very appropriate.
FINAL DISPOSITION: 1952: Retired and sold to Tahsis and Co. and converted to a barge. 1953: Sank.

PUYALLUP

BUILT: 1999, Todd Shipyard, Seattle, WA.
OFFICIAL NUMBER: D1061310 CALL SIGN: WCY7938
L/B/D: 460 x 90 x 17 GROSS/NET TONS: 6184/2066 PASSENGERS/AUTOS: 2499/202
PROPULSION: 4 EMD 16-710 G7 diesels, 13200 HP SPEED: 18 knots
NAME TRANSLATION: From the Puyallup language: "generous people." The Puyallup tribe had a reputation for generosity in dealing with traders and travelers. Early settler Ezra Meeker renamed his town from Franklin in 1877 looking for something unique. Besides the tribe and town, the name "Puyallup" is also used for a river and a glacier on Mount Rainier.
FINAL DISPOSITION: In service, 2019.

QUEEN OF BURNABY

BUILT: 1965, Victoria Machinery Depot, Victoria, British Columbia.
PREVIOUS/LATER NAMES: a. *Queen of Burnaby*, b. *Royal Victorian*, c. *Princess Marguerite III*, d. *Queen of Burnaby*
OFFICIAL NUMBER: 322978 CALL SIGN: VCVV
L/B/D: 399 x 75 x 17 GROSS/NET TONS: 4902/3346 PASSENGERS/AUTOS:659/192
NAME TRANSLATION: For the city of Burnaby, British Columbia, so named for after the legislator, speaker, Freemason and explorer Robert Burnaby.
FINAL DISPOSITION: Sold for scrapping in Ensenada, MX, 2018.

QUILCENE

BUILT/REBUILT: 1916/26/30 Joseph Supple, Portland, OR/Lake Washington Shipyard, Houghton, WA.
PREVIOUS/LATER NAMES: a. *Kitsap II*, b. *City of Bellingham*, c. *Quilcene*, d. *YHB-5*
OFFICIAL NUMBER: 214056

L/B/D: 146 x 43 x 13 **GROSS/NET TONS:** 401/272 **PASSENGERS/AUTOS:** 517/36

PROPULSION: 1 four-cylinder triple-expansion steam engine, 1200 **HP SPEED:** 14 knots

NAME TRANSLATION: After the tribe of the same name, which translates to "salt water people."

FINAL DISPOSITION: Sold to US Government, *YHB*-5. Sold to Freeman & Gibson, Seattle, WA, and converted to floating machine shop, 1947. No record of her exists after the report of sale; likely scrapped.

QUILLAYUTE

BUILT: 1927, Winslow Marine Railway and Shipbuilding Co. WA, for Sound Ferry Lines.

PREVIOUS/LATER NAMES: a. *Quillayute*, b. *Samson IV*

OFFICIAL NUMBER: 226513 (Canada: 193305)

L/B/D: 160 x 52 x 13 **GROSS/NET TONS:** 986/670 **PASSENGERS/AUTOS:** 600/36

PROPULSION: Washington Estep Diesel, 750 **HP SPEED:** 10 knots

NAME TRANSLATION: From the Quileute tribe and river of the same name, meaning "Joining together of rivers."

FINAL DISPOSITION: Scrapped, 2003.

HISTORY: June 23, 2003, while still in use as a fish camp moored in Naden Harbour, Graham Island, the *Quillayute's (*as the *Samson IV)* neighboring fish camp the *Pender Lady,* began to list. The Coast Guard rescued the people on board, but not before taking note of the *Quillayute's* condition. The next day, with the two vessels boomed off, the *Pender Lady* began to sink by the stern. Later in the afternoon, she had completely sunk in 55 feet of water. The *Pender Lady's* hull had been stuffed with foam plastic in order to maintain buoyancy and help keep her afloat. An inspection on the *Quillayute* revealed the old Black Ball ferry to be in a similar condition as the now sunken *Pender Lady,* including a hull stuffed with foam plastic to help keep the boat floating.

Fearing an even greater oil spill than the 2000 liters that had come from the *Pender Lady*, it was decided that both vessels should be disposed of to prevent further environmental damage—and that's exactly what happened. The *Pender Lady* was raised and broken up; the *Quillayute* towed to shore and broken up. What couldn't be salvaged was burned, ending over 75 years of service.

QUINAULT

BUILT/REBUILT: 1927/58/85 Moore Drydock Co., Oakland, CA/Commercial Ship Repair, Winslow, WA/ Seattle, WA .

PREVIOUS/LATER NAMES: a. *Redwood Empire*, b. *Quinault*

OFFICIAL NUMBER: 226738 **CALL SIGN:** WA9820

L/B/D: 256 x 74 x 13 **GROSS/NET TONS:** 1365/930 **PASSENGERS/AUTOS:** 616/59 cars (2007)

PROPULSION: Diesel-Electric, two Wartsila 824 TS diesels, **SPEED:** 12 knots

NAME TRANSLATION: From the Quinault language: "river with a lake in the middle." It refers to both the river and lake on the Olympic Peninsula.

FINAL DISPOSITION: Scrapped, Ensenada, MX, 2009.

RHODODENDRON

YEAR BUILT/REBUILT: 1947/90, Baltimore MD/Seattle, WA.

PREVIOUS/LATER NAMES: a. *Governor Herbert R. O'Conor*, b. *Rhododendron*

OFFICIAL NUMBER: 251646 **CALL SIGN:** WB6079

L/B/D: 227 x 62 x 10 **GROSS/NET TONS:** 937/425 **PASSENGERS/AUTOS:** 546/48 cars

PROPULSION: 2 Wartsila 624 TS diesels, 2172 **HP SPEED:** 11 knots

NAME TRANSLATION: State flower.

FINAL DISPOSITION: Retired in 2012 and sold to Island Scallops of Qualicum Beach, British Columbia, a branch of Atlantic Capes Fisheries of Cape May, New Jersey in 2013. She was used as a floating platform to handle scallops. Currently for sale. (2019)

ROSARIO

BUILT/REBUILT: 1923/31 Dockton, WA and Ballard Marine Railway Co. Seattle, WA.
PREVIOUS/LATER NAMES: a. *Whidby*, b. *Rosario*
OFFICIAL NUMBER: 223051 CALL SIGN: WPPQ
L/B/D: 156 x 41 x 9   GROSS/NET TONS: 290/197   PASSENGERS/AUTOS: 312/32
PROPULSION: Fairbanks Morse diesel, 600 HP   SPEED: 10 knots
NAME TRANSLATION: Spanish for rosary; a strait in the San Juan Islands, where the ferry sailed after rebuilding. Capt. Kellett gave it the present name in 1847 which is a simplification of the name Canal de Nuestra Senora del Rosario la Marinara, given in 1790 by Manuel Quimper.
FINAL DISPOSITION: Retired by Washington State Ferries in 1951. Sold in 1952 to Eugene Scheerer of Everett for use as a processing vessel. On register as late as 1981, the superstructure was bulldozed, and the hull buried under a parking lot on the Snohomish River.

SALISH

YEAR BUILT: 2011, Seattle, WA.
OFFICIAL NUMBER: 1229903 CALL SIGN: WDF6992
L/B/D: 274 x 64 x 11 GROSS/NET TONS: 4623/1887 PASSENGERS/ AUTOS: 750/64
PROPULSION: Diesel, variable pitch propeller, 6000 HP SPEED: 16 knots
NAME TRANSLATION: From Salishan: a group of people in the NW US and lower mainland Canada who speak a common language.
FINAL DISPOSITION: In service, 2019.

SAMISH

BUILT: 2015, Vigor Industrial, Seattle, WA.
OFFICIAL NUMBER: 1251777 CALL SIGN: WDH7552
L/B/D: 362 x 82 x 18 GROSS/NET TONS: 9292/3633 PASSENGERS/AUTOS: 1500/144
PROPULSION: 2 diesel engines, variable pitch propellers, 6000 HP SPEED: 17 knots
NAME TRANSLATION: Named for the Samish tribe, which means "giving people."
FINAL DISPOSITION: In service, 2019.

SAN DIEGO

BUILT: 1931, Moore Drydock Company, Oakland, CA.
OFFICIAL NUMBER: 231278 CALL SIGN: WK3851
L/B/D: 191 x 44 x 14 GROSS/NET TONS: 556/378 PASSENGERS/AUTOS: 500/50 cars
PROPULSION: 3 engines, 350 HP each
NAME TRANSLATION: Named for the city; vessel was built for the San Diego-Coronado ferry run. It derives from a re-analysis of Sant Yago (Saint James the Greater) as San Diego.
FINAL DISPOSITION: Scrapped, 2011.

SAN MATEO

BUILT: 1922, Bethlehem Steel Corporation, Union Yard, San Francisco, CA.
OFFICIAL NUMBER: 222386 CALL SIGN: WG5465
L/B/D: 230 x 64 x 12   GROSS/NET TONS: 919/625 PASSENGERS/AUTOS: 659/50
PROPULSION: triple expansion steam engine, 1400 HP SPEED: 13 knots
NAME TRANSLATION: For the California city, Spanish for "Saint Matthew."
FINAL DISPOSITION: Scrapping/abandoned on the Fraser River, British Columbia, Canada.

SEALTH

BUILT/REBUILT: 1982/2006 Marine Power & Equipment/Todd Shipyard, Seattle, WA.
OFFICIAL NUMBER: 662478 CALL SIGN: WAK7089
L/B/D: 328 x 78 x 16 GROSS/NET TONS: 2477/1772 PASSENGERS/AUTOS: 1200/90
PROPULSION: 2 GE 7 FDM-12 Diesels, 5000 HP SPEED: 16 knots
NAME TRANSLATION: The Native American/Chinook two-syllable pronunciation (*See-alth*) of Seattle, the chief of the Duwamish and Suquamish tribes who befriended early settlers in the 1850-60s.
FINAL DISPOSITION: In service, 2019.

SEATTLE

BUILT/REBUILT: 1909/24 Portland, OR/Seattle, WA.
PREVIOUS/LATER NAMES: a. *H.B Kennedy*, b. *Seattle*
OFFICIAL NUMBER: 206030
L/B/D: 185 x 44 x 11 GROSS/NET TONS: 504/343 PASSENGERS/AUTOS: 1000/47
PROPULSION: one four-cylinder triple-expansion engine, 2000 HP SPEED: 20 knots
NAME TRANSLATION: For the city of the same name (see *Sealth*).
FINAL DISPOSITION: Scrapped, 1939.

SHASTA

BUILT: 1922, Bethlehem Steel Corporation, Union Yard, San Francisco, CA.
PREVIOUS/LATER NAMES: a. *Shasta*, b. *Centennial Queen*, c. *River Queen Restaurant*
OFFICIAL NUMBER: 222598 CALL SIGN: WH6754
L/B/D: 230 x 64 x 12 GROSS/NET TONS: 919/625 PASSENGERS/AUTOS: 458/55
PROPULSION: Triple expansion steam engine, 1200 HP SPEED: 13 knots
NAME TRANSLATION: From the Cascade volcano in northern California (various meanings, one being "white mountain").
FINAL DISPOSITION: Scrapped by order of U.S. Coast Guard, summer 2018.

SKAGIT

BUILT: 1989, Halter Marine Shipyard, New Orleans, LA.
OFFICIAL NUMBER: D949140 CALL SIGN: WAA6309
L/B/D: 112 x 25 x 8 GROSS/NET TONS: 96/65 PASSENGERS/AUTOS: 230/0
PROPULSION: Diesel, 3840 HP SPEED: 25 knots
NAME TRANSLATION: From the tribe/river/county—name meaning lost.
FINAL DISPOSITION: Sold to a Canadian boat broker, who then resold the *Skagit* and sister *Kalama* to a ferry company in Tanzania for use between the mainland and Zanzibar. Sank while dangerously overloaded on 18 July 2012 with an *official* death toll of 144, but an *estimated* death toll of 293.

SKANSONIA

BUILT: 1929, Skansie Brothers Shipyard, Gig Harbor, WA.
OFFICIAL NUMBER: 229088 CALL SIGN: WA7467
L/B/D: 165 x 51 x 9 GROSS/NET TONS: 446/303 PASSENGERS/AUTOS: 465/32
PROPULSION: Fairbanks-Morse Diesel SPEED: 8 knots
NAME TRANSLATION: A play on the name of the builders, the Skansie Brothers.
FINAL DISPOSITION: In service, albeit stationary, as a wedding and event center on Lake Union.

SNOHOMISH

BUILT: 1999, Dakota Creek Industries, Anacortes, WA.
PREVIOUS/LATER NAMES: a. *Snohomish*, b. *Napa*
OFFICIAL NUMBER: 1084026 CALL SIGN: WDE8110
L/B/D: 149 x 39 x 5 GROSS/NET TONS: 99/67 PASSENGERS/AUTOS: 450/0
PROPULSION: Diesel waterjet SPEED: 36 knots
NAME TRANSLATION: Chinook for "tide water people."
FINAL DISPOSITION: In service in San Francisco, 2019.

SOL DUC

BUILT: 1912, Seattle Construction & Drydock, Seattle, WA
OFFICIAL NUMBER: 210133 SIGNAL LETTERS: LCKW
L/B/D: 189 x 32 x 23 GROSS/NET TONS: 1085/667 PASSENGERS/AUTOS: 453 day, 149 in cabins/11 cars
PROPULSION: One triple expansion engine, 1,500 HP SPEED: 15 knots
NAME TRANSLATION: Chinook for "sparkling, mystical waters."
FINAL DISPOSITION: Scrapped 1948.

SPOKANE

BUILT/REBUILT: 1972/2003, Todd Shipyard, Seattle WA.
OFFICIAL NUMBER: 544785   CALL SIGN: WYX2004
L/B/D: 440 x 87 x 16 GROSS/NET TONS: 3245/1198 PASSENGERS/AUTOS: 2000/188
PROPULSION: 4 EMD 16 710 G7 diesels SPEED: 18 knots
NAME TRANSLATION: Eastern Washington Native American tribe: "children of the sun" or "sun people." A city, county and river are also named after the tribe.
FINAL DISPOSITION: In service, 2019.

STEILACOOM (I)

BUILT: 1936 Bath Iron Works, Bath, ME.
PREVIOUS/LATER NAMES: a. *Aquidneck*, b. *Steilacoom*, c. *Point Ruston*
OFFICIAL NUMBER: 582707 CALL SIGN: WYL6353 (as *Point Ruston*)
L/B/D: 128 x 52 x 13 GROSS/NET TONNAGE: 420/285
HISTORY: Built by Bath Iron Works, Bath, ME (YN 167) as *Aquidneck* or *YFB-14* for the U.S. Navy. Laid down July 28, 1936, and launched February 13, 1937, the vessel went into service for the Navy on May 28, 1937, at Naval Torpedo Station, Newport, RI. The *Aquidneck* was taken out of service and place in reserve in October 1971, being struck from the Naval Register in July of 1975 and transferred to the Department of the Interior on November 1, 1975. The ferry was sold to Pierce County on December 19, 1975, for use on the Steilacoom-Ketron Island-Anderson Island run and renamed M/V *Steilacoom*. After reconditioning, the ferry finally went into service in August 1977, where it put the Islander into back-up status until the arrival of the *Christine Anderson*, which put the *Steilacoom* into back-up service.
NAME TRANSLATION: For the city of Steilacoom. One of the first towns founded in Washington, originally as Port Steilacoom by Lafayette Balch. There are several versions of the name origin, including that it originated from a Chief Tail-a-koom or that Lafayette Balch took the name from an existing creek that was spelled "Cheilcoom."
FINAL DISPOSITION: The *Steilacoom was* sold for $49,500 to R. T. Wallace of Haldo Inc., Las Vegas, NV, February 2007, and sold again on eBay to real estate developer Mike Cohen, renamed M/V *Point Ruston*, 2008. As of 2019, in use as a floating showroom and conference center for the Point Ruston condo development, Point Ruston, WA.

STEILACOOM II *(See above for name meaning.)*

BUILT: 2006, Nichols Brothers Boat Builders, Freeland, WA.
OFFICIAL NUMBER: 1192706 CALL SIGN: WDD5115
L/B/D: 197 x 68 x 10 GROSS/NET TONS: 97/66 PASSENGERS/AUTOS: 325/54
FINAL DISPOSITION: In service for Pierce County, 2019.

SUQUAMISH

BUILT: 2018, Vigor Industrial Shipyard, Seattle, WA.
OFFICIAL NUMBER: 1272842 CALL SIGN: WDJ9559
L/B/D: 362 x 83 x 24 GROSS/NET TONS: 3694/3323 PASSENGERS/AUTOS: 1500/144
PROPULSION: 2 x EMD 12-710G7C Diesel Engines SPEED: 17 knots
NAME TRANSLATION: From the tribe, "people of the clear salt water."
FINAL DISPOSITION: In service, 2019.

TACOMA (I)

BUILT: 1913, Seattle Construction and Drydock Company, Seattle, WA.
OFFICIAL NUMBER: 211198 SIGNAL LETTERS: LCWK
L/B/D: 221 x 30 x 18 GROSS/NET TONS: 836/458 PASSENGERS/AUTOS: 1000/0
PROPULSION: 4-cylinder triple expansion steam engine, 3500 HP SPEED: 22+ knots
NAME TRANSLATION: Derived from the native word Tah-ho-mah for Mt. Rainier, or "snowy mountain."
FINAL DISPOSITION: Scrapped, 1938.

TACOMA (II)

BUILT: 1997, Todd Pacific Shipyard, Seattle, WA.
OFFICIAL NUMBER: D1052576 CALL SIGN: WCX9244
L/B/D: 460 x 90 x 17 GROSS/NET TONS: 3926/2066 PASSENGERS/AUTOS: 2500/202
PROPULSION: 4 EMD 16-710 G7 diesels, 13200 HP SPEED: 18 knots
NAME TRANSLATION: See above.
FINAL DISPOSITION: In service, 2019.

TILLIKUM

BUILT: 1959/94 Puget Sound Bridge and Drydock Co., Seattle, WA.
OFFICIAL NUMBER: D278437 CALL SIGN: WL3377
L/B/D: 310 x 73 x 16 GROSS/NET TONS: 2069/1407 PASSENGERS/AUTOS: 1061/87
PROPULSION: 2 EMD 12-645-F7B diesels, 2500 HP SPEED: 13 knots
NAME TRANSLATION: Chinook for "friend."
FINAL DISPOSITION: In service, 2019.

TOKITAE

BUILT: 2014, Vigor Industrial Shipyards, Seattle, WA.
OFFICIAL NUMBER: 1251144   CALL SIGN: WDH3588
L/B/D: 362 x 83 x 24 GROSS/NET TONS: 9292/3633 PASSENGERS/AUTOS: 1500/144
PROPULSION: 2 x EMD 12-710G7C Diesel Engines SPEED: 17 knots
NAME TRANSLATION: Chinook, "nice day, pretty colors."
FINAL DISPOSITION: In service, 2019.

TYEE

BUILT: 1985, Nichols Brothers Boat Builders, Freeland, WA.
PREVIOUS/LATER NAMES: a. *Glacier Express* b. *Express* c. *Tyee* d. *Aqua Express* e. *Glacier Express*
OFFICIAL NUMBER: 693273 **CALL SIGN:** WTS7740 (as *Tyee*)
L/B/D: 87 x 31 x 9 **GROSS/NET TONS:** 87/59 **PASSENGERS/AUTOS:** 250/0
NAME TRANSLATION: "Chief."
FINAL DISPOSITION: Resold to her original owners, renamed *Glacier Express* and in use as a tour boat in Alaska. In service, 2019.

VASHON

BUILT: 1930 Lake Washington Shipyard, Houghton, WA.
OFFICIAL NUMBER: 229805 **CALL SIGN:** WB3763
L/B/D: 200 x 58 x 12 **GROSS/NET TONS:** 641/436 **PASSENGERS/AUTOS:** 645/ 90 cars (1930) 50 (1980)
PROPULSION: 6-cylinder Washington Estep Diesel, 930 **HP SPEED:** 10.5 knots
NAME TRANSLATION: From the island, which was named by Captain Vancouver for his friend, Captain James Vashon.
FINAL DISPOSITION: Sank in Johnson Cove, Alaska, after running aground. Parts of the vessel still visible in the Cove.

WALLA WALLA

BUILT: 1972, Todd Pacific Shipyard, Seattle, WA.
OFFICIAL NUMBER: 546382 **CALL SIGN:** WYX2158
L/B/D: 440 x 87 x 16 **GROSS/NET TONS:** 3246/1198 **PASSENGERS/AUTOS:** 2000/188
PROPULSION: 4 EMD 16-710-G7 diesels **SPEED:** 18 knots
NAME TRANSLATION: "Place of many waters."
FINAL DISPOSITION: In service, 2019.

WASHINGTON (I)

BUILT: 1908, Seattle, WA.
PREVIOUS/LATER NAMES: a. *Washington* b. *YHB-4*
OFFICIAL NUMBER: 204997
L/B/D: 160 x 43 x 10 **GROSS/NET TONS:** 323/219
PROPULSION: steam, 600 HP
NAME TRANSLATION: For the state/first president of the US.
FINAL DISPOSITION: Still afloat (as a warehouse) at the foot of Ewing Street in Seattle in 1967. Scrapped sometime after that.

WASHINGTON (II)

BUILT: 1923 at St. Helens, Oregon, for use on the Columbia River.
OFFICIAL NUMBER: 222912
L/B/D: 120 x 36 x 9 **GROSS/NET TONS:** 95/64
HISTORY: Purchased by Black Ball in 1930 from the Longview Ferry Company, the *Washington* was likely put out of work but the new Longview Bridge. Black Ball assigned her to the Mukilteo-Columbia Beach run. For the next eight years or so, the *Washington* provided service on the route with the converted steamer *Puget*. It seems that the open-decked *Washington* was primarily a secondary service vessel, working the busier summer schedule and occasionally into fall, but taking the winters off. By 1939, with Black Ball having absorbed the Kitsap

County Transportation Company and having purchased the first round of larger ferries from San Francisco, the smaller vessels began to disappear. The 1939 schedule notes the much larger ferry *Bainbridge* working the route.
FINAL DISPOSITION: Abandoned/scrapped 1942.

WENATCHEE

BUILT: 1998, Todd Pacific Shipyards, Seattle, WA.
OFFICIAL NUMBER: 1061309 CALL SIGN: WCY3378
L/B/D: 460 x 90 x 17 GROSS/NET TONS: 3926/2066 PASSENGERS/AUTOS: 2500/202 cars
PROPULSION: 4 EMD 16-710-G7 diesels, 13200 HP SPEED: 18 knots
NAME TRANSLATION: From the Yakima word *wenatchi* for "river flowing from canyon." When Lewis and Clark traveled through the Columbia River valley in 1803-1805, they mentioned the word *Wenatchee* in their journal, hearing of the river and the tribe living along its banks. A city, lake, river, and national forest are also named after the tribe.
FINAL DISPOSITION: In service, 2019.

WHATCOM CHIEF

BUILT: 1962.
OFFICIAL NUMBER: 288249 CALL SIGN: WT4561
L/B/D: 94 x 44 x 9 GROSS/NET TONS: 69/47
NAME TRANSLATION: For the Lake/Creek/former part of Bellingham. A Lummi word, it means "noisy water."
FINAL DISPOSITION: In service, 2019.

WILLAPA

BUILT: 1927, Bethlehem Shipbuilding Union Yard, San Francisco, CA.
PREVIOUS/LATER NAMES: a. *Fresno*, b. *Willapa*, c. *Fresno*
OFFICIAL NUMBER: 226344 CALL SIGN: WB4495
L/B/D: 256 x 65 x 13 GROSS/NET TONS: 1024/696 PASSENGERS/AUTOS: 1500/90
PROPULSION: Diesel, Busch-Sulzer 2800 HP SPEED: 15 knots.
NAME TRANSLATION: From the extinct Willapa tribe from Southwestern Washington. Meaning unknown.
FINAL DISPOSITION: Upper works scrapped November 2009; hull scrapped between 2012-14.

YAKIMA

BUILT/REBUILT: 1967/2000 National Steel & Shipbuilding Co., San Diego/Todd Shipyard, Seattle, WA.
OFFICIAL NUMBER: 5118223 CALL SIGN: WY2988 (1967) WCD7863 (2018)
L/B/D: 382 x 73 x 19 GROSS/NET TONS: 2705/1115 PASSENGERS/AUTOS: 2000/144
PROPULSION: 4 EMD 645 Diesel Electric, 8000 HP SPEED: 17 knots
NAME TRANSLATION: "To become peopled; black bears; people of the narrow river." A city, county and river are also named after the English spelling of the tribe.
FINAL DISPOSITION: In service, 2019.